CW00384456

Imn

Theory Redux

Series editor: Laurent de Sutter

Immaterialism
Objects and Social Theory

Graham Harman

polity

First published in 2016 by Polity Press

Polity Press
65 Bridge Street
Cambridge CB2 1UR, UK

Polity Press
350 Main Street
Malden, MA 02148, USA

ISBN-13: 978-1-5095-0096-3
ISBN-13: 978-1-5095-0097-0(pb)

A catalogue record for this book is available from the British Library.

Library of Congress Cataloging-in-Publication Data

Names: Harman, Graham, 1968- author.
Title: Immaterialism : objects and social theory / Graham Harman.
Description: Malden, MA : Polity, 2016. | Includes bibliographical references.
Identifiers: LCCN 2015043559 (print) | LCCN 2016005675 (ebook) | ISBN
  9781509500963 (hardback) | ISBN 9781509500970 (pbk.) | ISBN 9781509500994
  (Mobi) | ISBN 9781509501007 (Epub)
Subjects: LCSH: Object (Philosophy) | Sociology. | Social
  sciences--Philosophy.
Classification: LCC BD336 .H37 2016 (print) | LCC BD336 (ebook) | DDC
  111--dc23
LC record available at http://lccn.loc.gov/2015043559

Typeset in 12.5 on 15 pt Adobe Garamond by
Servis Filmsetting Ltd, Stockport, Cheshire
Printed and bound in the United Kingdom by Clays Ltd, St Ives PLC

For further information on Polity, visit our website:
politybooks.com

Contents

CONTENTS

Part One

Immaterialism

1. Objects and Actors

This is a book about objects and their relevance to social theory. Since the books in this series are intended to be concise, I have had to omit a great deal that some readers will regard as central. Influential theorists such as Michel Foucault and Niklas Luhmann appear briefly if at all, while Roy Bhaskar and Manuel DeLanda (both personal favorites) lost entire sections during the final cuts. Instead, the first part of the book will focus on Actor-Network Theory (ANT), which I regard as the most important philosophical method to emerge since phenomenology in 1900, and on New Materialism, the school of contemporary thought most often confused with my own position, Object-Oriented Ontology (OOO).

The track record of ANT in dealing with objects is decidedly mixed. In one sense it already incorporates objects into social theory as much as anyone could ask for. ANT offers a flat ontology in which anything is real insofar as it *acts*, an extremely broad criterion that grants equal initial weight to supersonic jets, palm trees, asphalt, Batman, square circles, the Tooth Fairy, Napoleon III, al-Farabi, Hillary Clinton, the city of Odessa, Tolkien's imaginary Rivendell, an atom of copper, a severed limb, a mixed herd of zebras and wildebeest, the non-existent 2016 Chicago Summer Olympics, and the constellation of Scorpio, since all are equally objects: or rather, all are equally *actors*. OOO could hardly be more inclusive of objects than ANT, and in some respects it is even less so. Yet in another sense ANT loses objects completely, by abolishing any hidden depth in things while reducing them to their actions. After all, you or I or a machine are not just what we happen to be doing at the moment, since we could easily be acting otherwise, or simply lying dormant, without thereby becoming utterly different things. Instead of replacing objects with a description of what they do (as in ANT) or what they are made of (as in traditional materialism), OOO uses the term "object" to refer to any entity that cannot be paraphrased in terms of either its components or its effects.

The search for an object-oriented social theory is motivated by the concerns of object-oriented philosophy (Harman 2010a, 93–104). The first postulate of this philosophy is that all objects are equally objects, though not all are equally real: we must distinguish between the autonomy of *real* objects and the dependence of *sensual* objects on whatever entity encounters them (Harman 2011). This differs from neighboring theories that grant equal reality, though not equal *strength*, to anything that acts or makes a difference in the world, with two good examples being the philosophical positions of Bruno Latour (1988) and much later Levi Bryant (2011). It is not hard to name social theorists who cast as wide an ontological net as Latour: Durkheim's rival Gabriel Tarde (2012) immediately comes to mind. But whereas object-oriented philosophy treats all sizes of objects equally and considers each as a surplus exceeding its relations, qualities, and actions, Tarde grants privilege to the tiniest "monadic" level of entities, while Latour is reluctant to concede more reality to objects than to their effects. (See Harman 2012a and Harman 2009, respectively.)

A good theory must ultimately draw distinctions between different kinds of beings. However, it must earn these distinctions rather than smuggling them in beforehand, as occurs frequently in the *a priori* modern split between human beings on one side and everything else on the other (see Latour 1993). This answers the question of why an object-oriented approach is desirable: a good philosophical theory should begin by excluding nothing. And as for those social theories that claim to avoid philosophy altogether, they invariably offer mediocre philosophies shrouded in the alibi of neutral empirical fieldwork.

Concerning the question of whether an object-oriented approach is new, it might seem at first that the theme of objects in social theory is a familiar mainstream topic. Science studies as a discipline, and not just ANT in the strict sense, has seemingly bent over backwards to integrate nonhuman elements into its picture of society.

Karin Knorr Cetina (1997) has a good deal to say about objects, though her primary interest is in what she calls "knowledge objects," and in general her objects are chaperoned by human beings rather than existing outside human contact. Consider also the following promotional blurb for the useful Routledge anthology *Objects and Materials*:

> There is broad acceptance across the Humanities and Social Sciences that our deliberations on the social need to take place through attention to practice, to object-mediated relations, to non-human agency and to the affective dimensions of human sociality. (Harvey et al. 2013)

This passage is typical of recent trends in assigning two, and only two, functions to objects: (a) objects "mediate relations," with the implication that what they mediate are relations between humans; (b) objects have "agency," meaning that they are important when they are involved in some sort of action. These are the two ostensibly pro-object insights bequeathed by ANT and related schools. Their praiseworthy aim was to free us from an older tradition in which society was viewed as a self-contained realm where humans did all the acting and objects were passive receptacles for human mental or social categories.

Yet these two key points, however welcome by comparison with what came before, are precisely those points where recent theories have not pushed far enough. To say that objects mediate relations is to make the crucial point that unlike herds of animals, human society is massively stabilized by such nonhuman objects as brick walls, barbed wire, wedding rings, ranks, titles, coins, clothing, tattoos, medallions, and diplomas (Latour 1996). What this still misses is that the vast majority of relations in the universe do not involve human beings, those obscure inhabitants of an average-sized planet near a middling sun, one of 100 billion stars near the fringe of an undistinguished galaxy among at least 100 billion others. If we forget that objects interact among themselves even when humans are not present, we have arrogated 50 percent of the cosmos for human settlement, no matter how loudly we boast about overcoming the subject–object divide. A truly pro-object theory needs to be aware of relations between objects that have no direct involvement with people. This brings us, in turn, to the still controversial point about the agency of objects. Whether we praise objects for their agency or brashly deny that they have any, we overlook the question of what objects are when *not* acting. To treat objects solely as actors forgets that a thing acts because it exists rather than existing because it acts. Objects are sleeping giants holding their forces in reserve, and do not unleash all their energies at once.

Since it cannot be assumed that readers of the present book are deeply familiar with OOO, it will now be necessary to repeat some points already known to readers of my previous books. Enough time will remain afterward to add new twists capable of surprising even the most grizzled OOO veteran.

2. The Dangers of Duomining

There are only two basic kinds of knowledge about things: we can explain what they are made of, or explain what they do. The inevitable price of such knowledge is that we substitute a loose para-phrase of the thing for the thing itself. Whether we speak of a poem, a corporation, a proton, or a mailbox, something is changed when we try to

replace an object with an account of its components or its effects, as literary critics have long
known. (See Brooks 1947.) In technical terms, the
attempt to paraphrase objects always amounts to
undermining, overmining, or duomining them
(Harman 2013).

An object is undermined if we explain it in
terms of its smaller constituents, by way of a
downward reduction. Western science was born
in undermining, when the pre-Socratic thinkers
of ancient Greece aspired to find the ultimate
root that explained the composition of mid- and
large-sized entities. Are all extant things made of
water, air, fire, atoms, number, a formless lump,
or something else altogether? Undermining has
remained the dominant method of physics but
is less common in social theory, which does not
work in the idiom of ultimate particles. A surprising counter-example is Tarde, who bases his
sociology on tiny monadic substances that form
larger beings only by grouping together under a
single dominant monad, rather than by forming a larger compound entity *per se* (Harman
2012a). Undermining can also occur when
authors emphasize the dependence of humans on
their background conditions, as in the landmark

New Materialist anthology of Diana Coole and Samantha Frost: "Our existence depends from one moment to the next on myriad micro-organisms and diverse higher species, on our own hazily understood bodily and cellular reactions and on pitiless cosmic motions, on the material artifacts and natural stuff that populate our environment" (Coole & Frost 2010, 1). The problem with undermining is that it cannot account for the relative independence of objects from their constituent pieces or histories, a phenomenon better known as *emergence*. An object is not equal to the exact placement of its atoms, since within certain limits these atoms can be replaced, removed, or shifted without changing the object as a whole. Nor is an object identical with the influences received from its environment, since some of these remain ineffectual while others prove decisive. Rome, Athens, and Istanbul might be the same cities as in ancient times despite complete population turnover and radical cultural and infrastructural change. An object is more than its components, and hence cannot be paraphrased successfully by way of downward reduction.

But the greater danger for the humanities and social sciences is the opposite one, *overmining*.

Here, rather than treating objects as superficial compared with their ultimate tiniest pieces, one treats them as needlessly deep or spooky hypotheses by comparison with their tangible properties or effects. Eighteenth-century empiricism tells us that the object is nothing but a bundle of qualities; contemporary thinkers say instead that the object is nothing but its relations or discernible actions. Latour is surely the most stimulating present-day thinker of overmining, as in his daring claim that "there is no other way to define an actor than through its actions, and there is no other way to define an action but by asking what other actors are modified, transformed, perturbed, or created" (Latour 1999b, 122). The problem with overmining is that it allows objects no surplus of reality beyond whatever they modify, transform, perturb, or create. In this way ANT unknowingly repeats the argument of the ancient Megarians, who claimed that no one is a house-builder unless they are currently building a house, a claim refuted by Aristotle in the *Metaphysics* (Aristotle 1999, Book Theta, Chapter 6). For if objects were nothing more than their current expression in the world, they could not do anything differently in the time that follows. No "feedback loop" can replace the need for an excess in things beyond their relations, since an object cannot absorb or respond to feedback unless it is *receptive*, and this requires that it be more than what it currently does. Just as we saw that an object is more than its components, we now see that it is less than its current actions. The author Harman who currently types these words in the University of Florida Library while wearing a black sweater is far too *specific* to be the Harman who will leave Florida next Sunday and can remove the sweater whenever he pleases.

It is rare to find undermining or overmining strategies in isolation. Usually they combine in mutual reinforcement, in a two-faced reduction known as *duomining* (Harman 2013). The earliest duominer in the West was Parmenides, who proclaimed a double cosmos with a single unified Being on one side and a truthless play of opinion and appearance on the other. Everything was either pure unified depth or pure variegated surface, with no intermediate room for genuine individual things. Another example is found in certain forms of scientific materialism, which ruthlessly undermine when they treat ultimate particles, fields, strings, or indeterminate "matter" as the ultimate layer of the cosmos, but then ruthlessly overmine when claiming that mathematics can exhaust the primary qualities of this genuine layer. (See Meillassoux 2008.)

Undermining, overmining, and duomining are the three basic forms of knowledge, and for this reason they cannot be avoided, to the extent that human survival hinges on acquiring such knowledge. Yet some disciplines are not forms of knowledge while still having considerable cognitive value. Works of art and architecture are misunderstood if we reduce them downward to their physical components or upward to their socio-political effects, despite occasional attempts within those disciplines to do just that. There is something in these works that resists reduction in either direction, pushing back against the literal paraphrase of which knowledge always consists (Harman 2012b). The same holds for philosophy, which began not with the pre-Socratics but with Socrates' un-ironic insistence that he knows nothing and has never been anyone's teacher, along with his perpetual refusal to accept any specific definition of anything at all. Insofar as every theory has a tendency to reflect philosophically on its own conditions, it must build the ultimate unknowability and autonomy of things into its consideration of them. In other words, the philosophical foundations of any theory cannot be a form of knowledge but must be a subtler, more indirect way of addressing the world.

3. Materialism and Immaterialism

Interest in objects is often confused with interest in "materialism," one of the most overly cherished words in present-day intellectual life. Though much of the prestige of this term stems from its long association with the Enlightenment and the political Left, it is striking how different today's materialism is from the old one of atoms swerving through the void. This difference is not always for the better. As Bryant notes in frustration, "materialism has become a *terme d'art* which has little to do with anything material. Materialism has come to mean simply that something is historical, socially constructed, involves cultural practices, and is contingent . . . We wonder where the materialism in materialism is" (Bryant 2014, 2). But while it may be hard to define New Materialism precisely, it is easy to list a group of theses defended by most of its proponents, including those who do not explicitly call themselves New Materialists:

AXIOMS OF NEW MATERIALISM

- Everything is constantly changing.
- Everything occurs along continuous gradients rather than with distinct boundaries and cut-off points.
- Everything is contingent.
- We must focus on actions/verbs rather than substances/nouns.
- Things are generated in our "practices" and therefore lack any prior essence.
- What a thing *does* is more interesting than what it is.
- Thought and the world never exist separately, and therefore "intra-act" rather than interact (see Barad 2007).
- Things are multiple rather than singular (see Mol 2002).
- The world is purely immanent, and it's a good thing, because any transcendence would be oppressive.

Though each of these theses is usually advanced with an air of gallant novelty, it is striking how mainstream they have become throughout the human sciences. What is unmistakable on the list above is a deep commitment to the *overmining* method, whose weakness – we have seen – lies in its inability to distinguish objects themselves from how they currently happen to be acting or otherwise manifesting in the world. To do justice to the reality of objects, we need a term to oppose overmining materialisms of this sort. Though a natural opposite to materialism exists in the term "formalism," this word is too closely linked with abstract logico-mathematical procedures of a sort that are foreign to the object-oriented method. For this reason, I propose *immaterialism* as an antonym for the approaches described above. Let this name serve to denote the following principles:

AXIOMS OF IMMATERIALISM
- Change is intermittent and stability the norm.
- Everything is split up according to definite boundaries and cut-off points rather than along continuous gradients.
- Not everything is contingent.
- Substances/nouns have priority over actions/verbs.

- Everything has an autonomous essence, however transient it may be, and our practices grasp it no better than our theories do.
- What a thing *is* turns out to be more interesting than what it does.
- Thought and its object are no more and no less separate than any other two objects, and therefore they interact rather than "intra-act."
- Things are singular rather than multiple.
- The world is not just immanent, and it's a good thing, because pure immanence would be oppressive.

Will this new list merely deliver us to the opposite vice of undermining? No, because immaterialism recognizes entities at every scale of existence without dissolving them into some ultimate constitutive layer. A specific Pizza Hut restaurant is no more or less real than the employees, tables, napkins, molecules, and atoms of which it is composed, and also no more or less real than the economic or community impact of the restaurant, its headquarters city of Wichita, the Pizza Hut corporation as a whole, the United States, or the planet Earth. All these entities sometimes affect and are affected by others, but they are never exhaustively deployed in their mutual influence, since they are capable of doing other things or even nothing at all (Zubíri 1980). Stated differently, though a relational metaphysics can only handle relations and not objects, a non-relational metaphysics can handle both, since it is able to treat relations adequately as new compound objects. Will the new list return us to some sort of reactionary, essentialist, naïve realism? No, because our essentialism is not reactionary and our realism is not naïve. For whereas the old essentialism thought it could *know* the essence of things and then use this knowledge for oppressive political purposes ("the Oriental peoples are essentially incapable of self-rule"), immaterialist essentialism cautions that the essence is not directly knowable and thus generates frequent surprises. And whereas naïve realism thinks that reality exists outside the mind and we can know it, object-oriented realism holds that reality exists outside the mind and we *cannot* know it. Therefore, we gain access to it only by indirect, allusive, or vicarious means. Nor does reality exist only "outside the mind," as if humans were the only entities with an outside. Instead, reality exists as a surplus even beyond the causal interactions of dust and raindrops, never fully expressed in the world of inanimate relations any more than in the human sphere.

Earlier I noted that Latour reduces objects upward to whatever they "modify, transform, perturb, or create," thus converting them into actions with nothing left in reserve. Yet there is a sense in which Latour is aware of this problem, and even addresses it in several different ways. Perhaps the most effective of these ways can be found in his political theory, which makes an effort to avoid the modern extremes of Power Politics and Truth Politics, and is ultimately just as suspicious of Hobbes as of Rousseau (Harman 2014a). Latour's interest in the "object-oriented" politics of Walter Lippmann and John Dewey, following the important doctoral work of Noortje Marres (2005), is motivated by his insistence that there is no political *knowledge*. The reason is that knowledge always tries to short-circuit the cosmopolitical struggle (Stengers 2010) through which human and nonhuman entities mutually determine one another. It does so either by invoking some supposed political truth (be it egalitarian or elitist) or the contrary claim that politics is merely about power rather than truth

(Latour 2013, 327). Another point where Latour resists the reduction of entities to knowledge can be found in his sparkling but little-read critique of materialism (Latour 2007). In the golden age of materialist dogma, he reminds us, "an appeal to a sound, table-thumping materialism seemed an ideal way to shatter the pretensions of those who tried to hide their brutal interests behind notions like morality, culture, religion, politics, or art." Yet this entailed "a rather idealist definition of matter and its various agencies" (Latour 2007, 138) since materialism assumed in advance that it knew what matter was: mathematizable primary qualities with a physical base, as opposed to the "surprise and opacity" (Latour 2007, 141) that invariably belong to the world. From this, Latour might have drawn a further lesson that would have cast doubt on the basic principle of ANT. Namely, once we speak of objects in terms of surprise and opacity, we cannot reduce them to their actions and relations any more than to their ultimate pieces. Actor-networks are simply the inverted form of atom-networks.

There is no alternative but to endorse an anti-duomining theory, of which object-oriented philosophy is so far the only strict example. In an age when all the intellectual momentum belongs to context, continuity, relation, materiality, and practice, we must reject the priority of each of these terms, focusing instead on an *immaterialist* version of surprise and opacity. Given the parallel failings of the undermining reduction, the opaque surprises in question must be due to fully formed individuals at every scale rather than to a pampered layer of ultimate particles, or to what Jane Bennett vividly but wrongly describes as "the indeterminate momentum of the throbbing whole" (Bennett 2012, 226).

4. Attempts to Evolve ANT

Though the work of ANT has been carried out with a thousand sickles, Michel Callon, Bruno Latour, and John Law are often listed as the co-originators of the method. This has not prevented them from publicly expressing misgivings about ANT. Latour has gone so far as to write that "there are four things that do not work with actor-network theory: the word actor, the word network, the word theory, and the hyphen!" (Latour 1999a, 15). Ironic or not, these words foreshadow a more sweeping departure from ANT in his book *An Inquiry Into Modes of Existence* (Latour 2013). There Latour muses about an imagined ethnographer who has just learned the tradecraft of ANT and reports that "to her great confusion, as she studies segments from Law, Science, The Economy, or Religion she begins to feel that she is saying almost the same thing about all of them: namely, that they are 'composed in a heterogeneous fashion of unexpected elements revealed by the investigation.'" Though the ethnographer moves "from one surprise to another . . . somewhat to her surprise, this stops being surprising . . . as each element becomes surprising in the same way" (Latour 2013, 35). His proposed cure for such monotony is not to abandon actors and networks, but to argue that networks come in at least 14 different kinds that only cross paths occasionally, and as a rule mistakenly. Far from disappearing, networks (now known as the mode of [NET]) continue to do half the work of his new theory, while the mode he calls "preposition" [PRE] opens the gates to the other 12 modes. The later Latour maintains his established relational model of actors, which continue to be defined exhaustively by their actions with nothing held in reserve. Any surplus in the things comes not from a hidden essential core, but from their simultaneous participation in all of the modes other than the one we happen to be considering at any given moment – though unlike Spinoza's "attributes," they are only 14 in number rather than infinite. Despite the importance of Latour's ongoing modes project, it cannot provide the tools for an immaterialist account of the world, which requires an attention to the non-relational depth of things outside any network.

Another attempt to radicalize ANT from within is made by Law and his prominent Dutch ally Annemarie Mol, in a joint effort that shares both the strength and weakness of New Materialism. After giving a largely sympathetic account of Latour and Steve Woolgar's *Laboratory Life* (Law 2004, 18–42), Law makes a bold claim for the purported advance beyond ANT made by Mol, and by extension himself: "Bar one subtle but devastating difference, [Mol's] position is similar to that of Latour and Woolgar. And the difference? It is that medical inquiry *may* lead to a single reality, *but this does not necessarily happen*" (Law 2004, 55). The medical reference is to Mol's influential *The Body Multiple* (2002), a case study purporting to show that atherosclerosis is not a single disorder, but many. For it is established differently in such practices as angiography, surgery, and the use of microscopes, and is witnessed differently through varying constellations of symptoms. Mol's claim is not that a single disease simply manifests differently in different contexts: the more radical claim of her work is that different disorders are *produced* when one employs different methods of detecting them. She cannot accept the notion of a single real world viewed according to a multitude of perspectives. Neither can Law, who regards this as a form of naïve realism that he repeatedly calls "Euro-American metaphysics" (Law 2004, *passim*). The term is unfortunate, since it combines drastic overgeneralization about the history of Western philosophy with crowd-pleasing insinuation that non-Western peoples possess superior wisdom. Nor should we applaud Law's claim that the ambivalence of reality and its multiple truths allows us to nudge our scientific findings in one direction or the other based solely on assumed political beneficence. For this implies a direct access to political truth by suitably progressive academics at the very moment that Law and Mol try to foreclose any straightforward sense of *scientific* truth (Law 2004, 40).

Among other problems, this marks a regression to the early ANT preceding Latour's break with Hobbes (Latour 1993): a time when ANT viewed "truth" with suspicion while letting "power" pass through the gates unanalyzed (Harman 2014a, 51–5). Law's claim that he and Mol make a "devastating" objection to Latourian ANT cannot be affirmed, since their objection merely amounts to an *extrapolation* of the hostility to enduring unified entities that is already one of the hallmarks of Latour's own work. If Latour were ever to assert the unity of atherosclerosis against Mol's multiple versions of the disease (already hard to imagine), this would be due only to the provisional blackboxing of the illness after long collective labor by medical researchers, not to some inherent realist unity in the disease itself.

Nonetheless, Law is both clear and daring in his attempt to reverse the whole of Western philosophy as he sees it. Above all, he holds, we must avoid the classic "Euro-American" biases, according to which reality (1) is outside us, (2) is independent of our actions and perceptions, (3) precedes us, (4) consists of definite forms or relations, (5) is constant, (6) is passive, (7) is universal (Law 2004, 24–5). The common link that unifies

Law's and Mol's rejections of these principles is the sizable role that both grant to humans in producing the reality once thought to lie solely outside us. There is no atherosclerosis-in-itself, no airplane *an sich*, no noumenal Zimbabwean water pump: instead, reality is performed or produced. It is "produced in relations," and held together by "practices" (Law 2004, 59). The evident clash between the simultaneous unity and multiplicity of any entity is not treated by Law and Mol as a dangerous discrepancy and then worriedly resolved, but is openly celebrated as the birth of a new ontology: "alcoholic liver disease may be understood as a *fractional object*. Differently enacted in the different practices in the different sites, those differences are managed in a way that *also* secures the continued possibility of the singularity of alcoholic liver disease at each particular location" (Law 2004, 75, emphasis modified). The word "also" stands here for a metaphysical labor of "management" that is never actually accomplished: an unresolved paradox rather than the streamlined *fait accompli* that Law suggests.

The central role granted to human practices in this ontology is coupled with an unapologetic relationism, both of these being overmining positions which hold that "realities are produced, and have life, in relations" (Law 2004, 59). But elsewhere the two authors team up to counter the ontology of networks with a new theory of indeterminate fluids (Mol & Law 1994), a blatant undermining move that cannot account for the relative independence of entities from their personal histories. In short, Body Multiple Ontology simply repeats the duomining tendencies found in New Materialism more generally. But while we cannot accept Law and Mol's extreme form of anti-realism – however "materialist" it claims to be – there is an important principle in their work worth preserving. Many realists mistakenly assume that reality is only real when it is free of human contamination, with the result that art, politics, and society are somehow regarded as less real than the blending of chemicals or the shifting of tectonic plates. It is easily overlooked that humans and their works are real objects in their own right, and that the atherosclerosis diagnosed in a Dutch hospital is no less real than the fusion of heavy elements in a supernova: but also *no more* real, we should be careful to note.

5. The Thing-in-Itself

An important feature of object-oriented philosophy is its insistence on the unpopular
thing-in-itself as a crucial ingredient in intellectual
life. Immanuel Kant's *Critique of Pure Reason*,
first published in 1781, was the most recent major
earthquake in Western philosophy (Kant 2003).
Everything since is in some way a response to
the new Kantian landscape. If Kant's innovations
were to be summarized in a single concept, his
thing-in-itself would surely be the best candidate.
Whereas past philosophy was *dogmatic*, believ-
ing it could attain the truth of things directly
through reasoning, Kant insists that human cog-
nition is finite and cannot reach the things as
they really are. These "noumena" can be thought
but not known. Humans have direct access only
to "phenomena," and thus philosophy becomes
a meditation not on the world, but on the finite
conditions through which humans can understand it: space, time, and the 12 categories of
understanding.

We have already seen the problem with
duomining. If we reduce an object downward to
its pieces, we cannot explain emergence; if we

reduce it upward to its effects, we cannot explain change. From here it is easy to see why we need the thing-in-itself as the reality that cannot be converted into either of the two basic forms of knowledge: what a thing is made of, what a thing does. After all, any claim that a thing is convertible into knowledge cannot account for the obvious and permanent difference between a thing and knowledge of it: if we had perfect mathematized knowledge of a dog, this knowledge would still not be a dog. It will be said that this is a "straw man" argument, since philosophers are obviously aware that knowledge is different from its object. Yet it is not a question of whether philosophers are personally "aware" of this, but of whether their philosophies sufficiently account for it. When pressed, those who think we know the dog directly will explain impatiently that they are not Pythagoreans, and that our knowledge is of the *form* of the dog while the dog itself is the same form inhering "in matter" (see Meillassoux 2012). But this highly traditional doctrine has already been exposed by Latour as an instance of "transport without transformation": as if the "same" form could be in the dog and then extracted from it by the mind without alteration.

Against this dogmatic version of formalism, we need to acknowledge that there can be no equivalence between any two forms. Things are simply not convertible into knowledge, or into any sort of access through our "practices," without significant transformation. The real problem with Kant is not his introduction of the things-in-themselves, but his notion that they haunt human beings alone, so that the tragic burden of finitude is shouldered by a single species of object. What Kant failed to note is that since any relation fails to exhaust its *relata*, every inanimate object is a thing-in-itself for every other as well. But since the present book is concerned with human societies, object–object interaction apart from humans is only a peripheral concern for us here.

Perhaps the most frequent complaint about the thing-in-itself is that it leaves us with nothing but a "negative theology." Consider the following remarks by my differently-minded friend, the prominent rationalist philosopher Adrian Johnston:

> [N]umerous post-idealists in the nineteenth and twentieth centuries end up promoting a facile mysticism whose basic underlying logic is difficult to

distinguish from that of negative theology. The unchanging skeletal template is this: there is a given "x;" this "x" cannot be rationally and discursively captured at the level of any categories, concepts, predicates, properties, etc. (Johnston 2013, 93)

Similar words are spoken by partisans of ANT, as when Latour complains about "whining" by defenders of the thing-in-itself (Latour 2013, 85). Yet there are several problems here. The first is that negative theology is rarely just negative, and is only sometimes fruitless. Even in the early medieval writings of Pseudo-Dionysius, that negative theologian *par excellence*, we find an explanation of the Christian Trinity that is anything but negative:

In a house the light from all the lamps is completely interpenetrating, yet each is clearly distinct. There is distinction in unity and unity in distinction. When there are many lamps in a house there is nevertheless a single undifferentiated light and from all of them comes the one undivided brightness. (Pseudo-Dionysius 1987, 61)

One need not believe in the Trinity to find this analogy marvelous. Such examples will surely not sway Johnston, an atheist and materialist who is perfectly happy to leave theologians to what he sees as empty games. Yet Johnston's view of knowledge cannot account for something much dearer to him: philosophy itself. Recall his sarcastic words: "There is a given 'x;' this 'x' cannot be rationally and discursively captured at the level of any categories, concepts, predicates, properties, etc." But notice that this phrase equally describes the methods of Socrates. In what passage of what Platonic dialogue does Socrates ever "capture" anything at the level of categories, concepts, predicates, or properties? Socrates claims not to be a wise man, but a philosopher: a *lover* of wisdom. If anything distinguishes philosophy from the sciences, it is this claim to a non-knowledge that is nonetheless not just negative.

Johnston seems to think of knowledge as an all-or-nothing affair: either we know something in clear propositional language, or we are left with nothing but vague gesticulations. This false alternative is known as "Meno's Paradox," after Meno's statement to Socrates that we cannot look for something if we have it or if we do not, and hence that there is no reason to search for anything. This unphilosophical claim is countered by

Socrates with a most philosophical one: we neither have nor do not have the truth, but are always somewhere in between. Notice that Johnston's all-or-nothing view of intellectual activity is further unable to account for cognitively valuable activities that are not primarily conceptual or discursive. The arts are perhaps the best example of this. How can we paraphrase Picasso's *Les demoiselles d'Avignon* in discursive terminology without losing something crucial? If the best art critics write allusively and elliptically, this is not because they are "facile mystics" or irrational frauds, but because their subject matter demands nothing less. Good writing is not just clear and devoid of "fuzziness": it must also be *vivid* writing that brings its subject to life rather than replacing it with bundles of explicit and verifiable qualities. Sometimes we can only reveal things obliquely, looking for paradox rather than literally accurate predicates as our entryway to a thing.

Let us also put to rest another common prejudice about the thing-in-itself: the notion that it is "otherworldly." In fact, the immaterialist model acknowledges no duality of worlds. Rather, the point is that each object in *this* world is a thing-in-itself, since it cannot be translated without energy loss into any sort of knowledge, practice, or causal relation. We ourselves are things-in-themselves while inhabiting this very world, and so too are tables, hyenas, and coffee cups. Our immaterialist objection to "immanence" is not that it forecloses some utopian true world, but that pure immanence cannot account for change, and therefore leads to the notion that what is currently expressed in the world is all the world has to offer.

Having made some critical remarks about ANT and New Materialism and distinguished both of them from OOO, we should now consider a case study of an object. For reasons to be explained shortly, the long-vanished Dutch East India Company is an ideal example for our purposes.

Part Two

The Dutch East India Company

6. Introducing the VOC

The philosopher G. W. Leibniz was a deter-
mined but ambiguous champion of objects in
philosophy, under the famous name of "monads"
(Leibniz 1989, 213–24). Among other problems
with his theory, Leibniz insists on an absolute
distinction between simple, natural substances
on one side and compound, artificial aggregates
on the other. Whereas ANT is flexible enough
to analyze everything from trains to warheads
to hardening of the arteries, Leibniz brusquely
rejects the possibility that complex aggregates
could ever count as individual things. This is clear
from his correspondence in the 1680s with the

celebrated Jansenist theologian Antoine Arnauld. As Leibniz puts it there: "the composite made up of the diamonds of the Grand Duke and of the Great Mogul can be called a pair of diamonds, but this is only a being of reason" (1989, 85–6). That is to say, a "pair" of diamonds can be posited by the mind but under no circumstances can it count as a real thing. Leibniz continues the thought: "If a machine is one substance, a circle of men holding hands will also be one substance, and so will an army, and finally, so will every multitude of substances" (1989, 86). Simply put, he worries that any acknowledgment of machines, circles of men, or armies as real would put us on the slippery slope to insisting that *any* random assortment of things must also count as a substance. For Leibniz the problem persists even if we use physical contact as our criterion for objecthood: "why should several rings, interlaced so as to make a chain, compose a genuine substance any more than if they had openings so that they could be separated?" (1989, 89). Using formal arrangement as our criterion of unity is no better, since "if parts fitting together in the same plan are more suitable for composing a true substance than those touching, then all the officers of the Dutch East India Company will make up a real substance, far better than a heap of stones" (1989, 89).

Leibniz intends this last point as a proof by *reductio ad absurdum*, as if the notion of the Dutch East India Company as a substance were so patently ridiculous that no one could ever take it seriously. But the unity of this object is precisely what I aim to defend. The Dutch East India Company is known in the Netherlands as the *Vereenigde Oostindische Compagnie* ("United East India Company"). The name is often shortened by scholars to its Dutch abbreviation VOC, and I will follow this handy convention. The company's official existence lasted from 1602 to 1795, though such dates should always be viewed as provisional. As a European power in Southeast Asia, the Dutch were preceded by Portuguese dominance and followed by a period of British hegemony. The Portuguese themselves intruded upon an era of Malay Sultans and local island governments, while the Dutch and British were followed by an independent Indonesia and Malaysia, respectively. When Western Empires are discussed in our time, exploitation and domination are usually the first thoughts on everyone's minds, and too often the only thoughts. In what follows, we will encounter cases of injustice and cruelty that no nation should aspire to repeat. Yet we should also not exaggerate European dominance, given the failure of Western powers to make hegemonic inroads in Tokugawa Japan (Clulow 2014) and especially Qing China (Willis 2005), and given further the enduring leverage of local sultanates in Aceh (in northern Sumatra) and Johore (in the Malay peninsula) during the lifespan of the VOC.

Based in Amsterdam, the VOC was the world's first joint-stock company, and hence gave rise to the world's first stock exchange. Whereas previous spice journeys were made by *ad hoc* companies set up by investors and dissolved once the ships returned to port, the VOC maintained a permanent fleet and a long-term pool of shareholders, not all of them wealthy. Due to the distance of Southeast Asia from the Netherlands and the slow communications of the time, the VOC was granted independent operating authority. Thus it effectively functioned as a sovereign state, empowered to wage wars, sign treaties, and administer often harsh justice in the name of the Netherlands itself. At the root of the VOC's successes and crimes was its status as a monopoly, which was necessary to keep prices high enough to support such an expensive overseas venture. The grim VOC Governor-General Jan Pieterszoon Coen would eventually argue that the very survival of the Dutch Republic required that this monopoly exclude other European powers in the most rigorous fashion (Brown 2009, 33). Beyond this, Coen's vision entailed further Dutch monopoly even on the intra-Asian spice trade. This would force the people of the East Indies into an exclusive arrangement with the VOC, thereby ruining their longstanding ties with Arab, Chinese, and Indian merchants, now reduced to dangerous smuggling arrangements. The VOC forced local people to resettle at locations convenient for its own operations, drove many into outright slavery, and destroyed vast numbers of trees to ensure that spices were grown only in locations firmly under VOC control.

Though some historical detail will be needed to bring the VOC to life for the reader, this book is not a history. Historians consult documents and other sources in an effort to determine what really happened in the past. The present book, for lack of a better term, is an *ontology* rather than a

history of the VOC. We will be less concerned
with what occurred than with the various key
entities that were on the scene, quite apart from
what came of them. If history is analogous to
the plot of a novel, ontology is more like a study
of the novel's central characters, whether they
be human, corporate, or inanimate. While ANT
always advises us to "follow the actors," object-
oriented theory is also interested in following the
dogs that did not bark, or the barking dogs at
moments when they slept. If ANT asks us to
follow controversies to grasp the moment when
things are incipient rather than ready-made, we
are also interested in the moments of uncontro-
versial reality in things, and of simple success
and failure rather than controversy. And if New
Materialist assemblage theory asks us to view
actors as in a state of constant change (Harman
2014b), the immaterialist method views most
change as superficial, and generally finds important change in cases of *symbiosis*, a concept to be
explained shortly.

In the common understanding, the word
"object" often means entities that are inanimate,
durable, nonhuman, or made of physical matter.
We have seen that immaterialism opposes such

criteria, and holds that an entity qualifies as an object as long as it is irreducible both to its components and its effects: that is to say, as long as the object is not *exhausted* by undermining or overmining methods, though of course these methods often yield fruits of their own. Seen in this light, the objecthood of the VOC seems beyond any reasonable doubt: though we must always remain open to possible evidence that suggests, say, that the single name of the company serves to conceal what was in fact three or four independent though simultaneous operations. Each of the ships in the VOC's mighty fleet can certainly be considered an object, but in no way is that fleet just an aggregate of individual ships, any more than each ship is just an aggregate of planks and maritime implements. The VOC meets the useful criteria put forth by DeLanda (2006) for identifying a real assemblage, his parallel term for what I call "object." (1) The VOC clearly has a retroactive effect on its parts: changing the lives and careers of its employees, reducing islanders to slavery, provoking the redesign and fortification of Asian territories, diverting spice to and from unprecedented cities. (2) The VOC just as clearly generates *new* parts: fleets specially ordered and designed for its needs, new trade outposts, and new coinage stamped with the company's emblem. (3) The VOC also has emergent properties not found in its components. Taken individually, the many soldiers and ships of the VOC would pose little threat to English shipping or the villagers of the Moluccas; once organized, however, the unified VOC is a fearsome and often vengeful war-machine. Yet we should emphasize that these retroactive effects, new parts, and visible emergent properties are merely symptoms that an object is present, and that none is a *sine qua non* for objecthood. For first of all, the VOC is not equal to its sum total of effects on its pieces, since it might always have different effects or possibly no effect on those parts. And second, a new object may be present without any discernible new properties meeting the eye, which happens especially in the case of what I call "dormant objects" (Harman 2010b), which exist despite a temporary or permanent state of not affecting anything at all.

7. On Symbiosis

Object-oriented philosophy is a realist position that views objects of every sort as existing prior to their relations or effects. Atherosclerosis and tuberculosis are not produced *ex nihilo* in the medical practices that first register their existence; rather, these diseases as encountered in practice transform some genuine pre-existent entity or entities that our experience translates more or less capably. Otherwise, we would find ourselves in an ontology so "immanent" as to be outright ideal-ist, and there would be no unexpressed surplus in the world able to give rise to change. When Mol treats "atherosclerosis" as the correlate of a particular diagnostic practice rather than as a disease-in-itself, this cannot be taken in the literal sense (though Mol evidently means it thus) that there is no such object apart from the practices that register its existence, something that happens only in cases of misdiagnosis. Instead, it should be viewed as a *synecdoche* in which a new compound object (doctor-plus-disease) is given the name of just one of its parts (the disease). In this way we are able to do justice to the effects of humans on the objects they contend with by treating such relations as new objects, however fleeting. What we must not do is decapitate all talk of the disease in its own right, as if illness existed only as the retroactive sidekick of human medical officials.

It would be strange to claim that a new *doctor* automatically comes into existence once athero-sclerosis is detected in his or her practices; we should view it as equally strange to think that the disease itself is first born at the moment when humans detect it. Latour often ventures such claims, as in his understandable view that Pasteur and the microbe co-create each other, given the vastly different life-path Pasteur took from that moment forward. Yet it is no accident that Latour chooses a *crucial* moment of Pasteur's career in making this claim, and never argues that Pasteur and his razor or doorknob co-create each other every morning, though such extreme claims are no less implicit in his relational ontol-ogy. If all relations were equally significant, then every entity would become a new thing in every trivial instant of its existence, since our relations with objects are ever on the move. Yet it is equally problematic if someone agrees with us that *not* all relations are equally important, but then goes on to employ an arbitrary external standard for what counts as important: "significance for human practice," for instance. If we wish to avoid the absurdity of treating all cataclysmic and frivolous events as equally decisive in the life of an object,

we need a standard that can isolate those relatively rare events that transform an object's very
reality.

If we treat every relation as significant for its
relata, we slip into a "gradualist" ontology in
which every moment is just as important as every
other. In evolutionary biology, one prominent
way of countering excessive gradualism is the
theory of punctuated equilibrium (Eldredge &
Gould 1972). Here, rather than species evolv-
ing gradually through random genetic variation
and the slightly higher death rate of weaker
individuals, evolution occurs through sudden
leaps interspersed with longer periods of relative
stability. This makes a good start for immaterialist theory. Yet the implications of punctuated
equilibrium could still prove too event-oriented
for our purposes, since the sudden changes in
species might be spun as resulting mainly from
cataclysmic environmental change, as with the
famous Yucatan asteroid that may have killed off
the dinosaurs. Thus, a better model for us can
be found in the Serial Endosymbiosis Theory of
Lynn Margulis (a.k.a. Lynn Sagan), the leading
proponent of the theory that the organelles inside
eukaryotic cells were once independent creatures

before later becoming subordinate components of the unified cell (Sagan 1967; Margulis 1999). One of the highlights of this theory, initially ignored or rejected before being enshrined as textbook biology, is its suggestion that the gradual shaping of the gene pool through natural selection is a less important evolutionary force than the watershed symbioses of distinct organisms. The idea has obvious value beyond the sphere of evolutionary biology: in human biography, for instance. We find that the key moments in a human life rarely result from introspective brooding in one's private chambers. Instead, they happen most often through symbiosis with a person, a profession, an institution, a city, a favorite author, a religion, or in some other life-changing bond. Even in those cases where great events do happen inside one's private head, this takes the form of symbiosis with a crucial idea or decision to which one is henceforth dedicated. Despite the co-operative-sounding etymology of the term, symbiosis is often non-reciprocal: it is easy to recognize moving to Cairo in the year 2000 as a turning-point in my own life, without being tempted by narcissistic delusions that Egypt's storied capital entered a new stage upon my arrival. In any case, like other social objects, humans have neither one life nor many, but *several* in succession.

What the model of symbiosis suggests is that both of the usual alternatives are wrong: entities have neither an eternal character nor a nominalistic flux of "performative" identities that shift and flicker with the flow of time itself. Instead, we should think of an object as going through several turning-points in its lifespan, but not many. Some of these will be historically noisy, such as major battles, the ascent of a tyrant, or love at first sight. Yet some noisy events prove not to be crucial, while symbiosis may occur quietly with a brief or long delay before its impact is registered on the environment. This shifts the emphasis away from actors and actions, while providing new tools to take objects seriously even when they are not acting. Part of the widespread appeal of Alain Badiou's philosophy stems from his powerful intuition that events are relatively rare (Badiou 2006). Yet Badiou is a modernist and idealist who roots such events too one-sidedly in the fidelity of the human subject, in keeping with the dose of existentialism he absorbed from Kierkegaard and Sartre. Against this we must recognize that symbiotic change is not always a question of human devotion, since it affects even the lazy shuffler who may not remain faithful to the love affair, religious conversion, political revolution, or business merger he has perhaps entered irreversibly anyway. We can still appreciate Badiou's wish to quantize history rather than embracing the constant flow of movement for movement's sake, which he rightly dismisses as futile. Yet immaterialism holds that Badiou's human wagers on the importance of a vanished event are not the best criteria for turning-points in the lives of entities. We must look instead for symbioses that mark genuine points of irreversibility, whether or not the subject is lucid, euphoric, resolute, or heroic when they occur.

Readers might also wonder how my use of "symbiosis" differs from that of Gilles Deleuze. In his dialogues with Claire Parnet we read as follows: "the assemblage's only unity is that of a co-functioning: it is a symbiosis, a 'sympathy.' It is never filiations which are important, but alliances, alloys; these are not successions, lines of descent, but contagions, epidemics, the wind" (Deleuze & Parnet 2002, 69). Whatever Deleuze really means by symbiosis, it is clear from this passage that he means it in a broader sense than

OOO does. If every alliance and alloy (not to mention contagions, epidemics, and the wind) is enough to count as a symbiosis, then Deleuze cannot help us at this juncture, since our purpose with the term "symbiosis" is to *narrow down* ANT's already broad concept of relations. We use it instead to refer to a special type of relation that changes the reality of one of its *relata*, rather than merely resulting in discernible mutual impact.

I have spoken of symbiosis as the central concept of immaterialist theory, and implied that each new symbiosis in the life of an object gives rise to a *stage*; we use this term rather than "phase," which DeLanda already employs in a different sense when he borrows the term "phase-changes" from natural science. There are also *pseudo-symbioses* in which a noisy event is mistaken for a symbiosis, and which bear some resemblance to Badiou's under-theorized notion of "pseudo-events" (Badiou 2006). More important here is an apparent ambiguity in the concept of symbiosis itself. Margulis uses this term to refer to the emergence of full-fledged new species. In a seemingly different manner, immaterialism proposes symbiosis as the key to unlocking a finite number of distinct phases in the life of the same object rather than the creation of a new one. Without the concept of symbiosis, we would be left philosophically with one of three undesirable outcomes: (1) A gradualist account of the life of an object in which all moments are dramatically equivalent no matter how important or trivial they may be; (2) a non-gradualist model that accepts the difference between trivial and important phases in an object, but only by using the extrinsic criterion of how much effect these changes have on outside objects; (3) an alternative theory of symbiosis that treats each phase of the VOC as a brand new object, thereby foreclosing any effort to establish discrete stages in its life, and driving us back into a local use of position (1) or (2) for each object.

If symbiotic stages are meant to mark discrete phases in the life of one and the same object, they must of course be distinguished from the birth and death of objects. In order to focus for now on stages, we will provisionally accept the official start and end dates of the VOC. The birth of the VOC seems to occur in 1602 with the official formation of the company as an autonomous monopoly for the Dutch spice trade, and its death apparently happens late in 1795 with the nationalization of the VOC by the Dutch government, freshly under Napoleonic control. We should now determine the chief stages that occur between the company's provisional birth and death. Neither ANT nor New Materialism can help us here, since we seek both the VOC-object apart from its actions and an explicitly "chunky" periodization of its existence in time.

8. Governor-General Coen

One of the recurring intellectual tropes of the past century is the notion that things must be replaced with actions, static poses with dynamic processes, nouns with verbs. From Bergson and James, through Whitehead and certain dynamicist readings of Heidegger, all the way up to more recent Deleuzian currents, "becoming" is blessed as the permanent trump card of innovators, while "being" is cursed as a sad-sack regression to the archaic philosophies of olden times. OOO chooses to emphasize the opposite principle: not because becoming is illusory, but only because transient process cannot occur without something withheld from the process. Numerous authors still maintain that "what a thing can do" is more important than the question of "what it is," including Bryant (2014, 17). If we stress the word "can," the phrase "what a thing *can* do" at least takes a step beyond the theory that an entity is only what it actually does right now: a step analogous to Aristotle's surpassing of the Megarians through his concept of potentiality. Yet this purported advance still assumes that at the end of the day, nothing matters aside from what sort of *impact* a thing has or might eventually have on its surroundings. This risks obscuring our view of objects in a number of ways, which not only poses[1] an ontological problem, but has methodological consequences as well. For instance, if we misinterpret the VOC as consisting of "what it can do" rather than "what it is," we will tend to overreact to the most histrionic incidents during its lifespan, since these are the most vivid examples of "doing" that a thing can provide. More specifically, any provisional list of the highlights and lowlights of "what the VOC can do" is likely to over-emphasize great ceremonies, battles, weddings, treaties, massacres, annexations, and discoveries. This may be the correct strategy if what we seek are the moments of the company's maximum historical impact. Yet we are not interested here in every VOC incident that was important to various lucky or unlucky objects, but only in those that were important to the VOC itself.

Though symbiosis can certainly be described in verbs once it has occurred, the heart of the concept is a connection between two objects, expressed linguistically as nouns. Just to get the ball rolling, let's provisionally adopt the old schoolhouse classification "a noun is a *person*, *place*, or *thing*," not worrying for now as to whether this distinction is purely arbitrary, or whether it has a solid foundation that can do real intellectual work for us. At this point we are simply organizing the available information about the VOC. Working in the traditional order, let's start with the "person" type of noun. Quite often in the humanities and social sciences, arguments over the role of people come down to the question of whether we emphasize dramatic contributions by great individuals or the piecemeal teamwork of collectives. Which side one chooses often seems to be tacitly correlated with the elitist or egalitarian political instincts, respectively, of whoever happens to be speaking. The problem is that whether we think history revolves around individuals or collectives, both options deal in the anthropocentric currency of *people*. Immaterialism trades instead in the coin of *objects*, and this often makes it possible to view the different careers of humans as variant responses to an underlying object. For example, important European philosophers often appear in groups of three or four: presumably not because human genetic endowment surges in specific historical periods, but more likely because there are several different ways to formulate an underlying new idea that takes hold of an epoch. In this way, both individuals and collectives are less important than the objects with which they bond.

Yet it is often wrongly assumed that OOO, with its focus on objects, must reach those objects by expelling or exterminating humans. Many of the misleading questions addressed to OOO make this same false assumption: "What would an art without humans be like?"; "What would an architecture without humans look like?" The point is not to *subtract* humans from any given situation, but to focus on the way that humans are themselves *ingredients* in a symbiosis rather than just privileged observers looking on from the outside. We must remember that humans themselves are objects, and that they are richer and more momentous as objects the more they are not the mere product of their time and place, but push back against whatever circumstances they face. For this reason, when considering a symbiosis, we may as well begin by looking for outstanding individual humans in the history of the VOC. This cuts against the grain of fashions that lament the "great man" theory of history and "the Romantic conception of genius," as if anything spawned by Romanticism were inherently false. Recent trends have focused more on the study of everyday life and gradual collective achievements than on traditional top-down tales of kings and captains and their treaties and battles, and there is an often unstated assumption that progressive democratic politics demands nothing less. And indeed, it is true that an object such as the Dutch East India Company could never have come into being if not for certain collective features found in the Netherlands: the outstanding maritime and shipbuilding skills of the Dutch people, the existential threat posed to the new country by its former Spanish masters, the soaring personal and national aspirations of the Dutch people as a whole at that moment in history. But while such factors are decisive in the

birth of the VOC, we are now speaking instead
of its symbiotic transformation, and symbiosis
involves an element of chance more easily linked
with the peculiarities of a given person than with
broader collective properties. Stated differently,
we begin with a hunt for remarkable individuals
only because the proximate source of a new stage
is more often linked with the idiosyncratic vision
or will of one person than the statistical average
of a committee or nation. For these are generally among the background conditions already
factored into the *status quo* rather than proximate
causes or catalysts for changing it.

In surveying the full history of the VOC,
the most outstanding personality is clearly Jan
Pieterszoon Coen (1587–1629), who counts today
as a classic imperialist villain (Brown 2009, 9–55).
A ghoulishly ambitious figure who proved capable of racketeering and massacre in a mood of
stern Calvinist piety, Coen served two terms as
Governor-General of the VOC (1618–23 and
1627–9), separated by a brief period of resi-
dence in Amsterdam. In the words of Stephen
R. Brown, "Coen certainly believed that the use
of violent force was the only path to prosper-
ity for the VOC. An accountant by training, he

proved to be a master tactician and a ruthless strongman" (Brown 2009, 31). Of the numerous dramatic incidents in Coen's career, the following 12 would seem to be the most noteworthy for any biographer:

- 1609: The young Coen witnesses the ambush and massacre of Admiral Pietrus Verhoefen and other VOC personnel by inhabitants of the Spice Island of Banda, following ill-received VOC demands for a trade monopoly.
- 1613: Coen exchanges insults on the Spice Island of Ambon with Commander John Jourdain of the English East Indies Company (EIC), with Coen telling Jourdain that the English have no right to be there.
- 1614: Coen authors his infamous *Discourse on the State of India*, which lays out a sweeping vision of total VOC monopoly on the East Indies trade. Despite some misgivings in liberal Amsterdam over its dark political implications, the *Discourse* is more or less accepted as a new blueprint for the company.
- 1616: Coen threatens the EIC garrison on the Spice Island of Ai, leading to their evacuation and easy VOC conquest of the island,

with the English retaining the nearby island of Run.

- 1618: Following the resignation of his superior, Coen is promoted to VOC Governor-General at the age of 31. Dutch and English soldiers fight in the streets of Banten in northwestern Java, where both have trading posts. Coen moves the VOC headquarters to Jayakarta (Jakarta), roughly 50 miles to the east.

- 1619: Coen orders the burning of the English trading post in Jayakarta. An EIC fleet commanded by Sir Thomas Dale then blockades the city and a ferocious naval battle ensues, with the English initially victorious. Coen flees eastward with his ships after ordering his soldiers in Jayakarta to defend their position. Dale does not pursue Coen and soon takes his fleet to India, whereupon Coen returns and orders a crushing assault on the whole of Jayakarta, which he renames "Batavia" after the Dutch fortress there. He is enraged when ordered by the VOC in Amsterdam to respect a new truce with the EIC that grants the VOC two-thirds of the spice trade and the already defeated EIC the remaining one-third.

- 1621: Coen returns to Banda to avenge the

massacre of Verhoefen's party 12 years earlier. Upon arrival, Coen swears at and shoves an Englishman who proposes peace between the VOC and the islanders. He has 45 leaders of Banda grotesquely tortured and executed by Japanese mercenaries, much to the chagrin of his own VOC men. Most surviving Bandanese are rounded up and shipped to Batavia to be sold into slavery.

- 1623: Coen's policy is to extirpate all nutmeg trees outside the VOC's area of control, and to convert the Banda Islands into a monopoly plantation system worked by slaves and overseen by Dutch planters selling to the VOC at low fixed prices.

- 1623: Coen ends his first term as Governor-General. Before leaving for Amsterdam he advises his lieutenant in Ambon, Herman van Speult, to keep a close eye on the small English contingent there. Warming quickly to his task, van Speult claims to discover conspiracy. He brutally tortures and executes a number of English, Japanese, and Portuguese, including his own frequent dinner companion, the English commander Gabriel Towerson. This incident ends the 1619 joint agreement between the VOC and the EIC, and tarnishes the VOC's reputation in Europe for decades.

- 1627: Coen arrives in Batavia for his second term as Governor-General. He withstands a lengthy siege by the rising Mataram Empire of Sultan Agung.
- 1628: Sultan Agung attacks again, this time with overwhelming force. But Coen uses VOC naval superiority to destroy the Mataram grain barges, thereby starving Agung's army into defeat.
- 1629: Saartje Specx, Coen's 12-year-old Dutch-Japanese ward (and colleague's daughter), is caught *in flagrante delicto* with a 15-year-old Dutch soldier. Coen has the soldier beheaded and Saartje publicly whipped, after initially resolving to have her drowned. Coen dies in Batavia of either dysentery or cholera at the age of 42. He is replaced as Governor-General by, of all people, Saartje's father Jacques Specx.

There is much here to excite both interest and dismay. If we focus on actions, on "what Coen does" or "what the VOC does" rather than on what they are, all of these incidents are of tremendous importance, and most would count as turning-points in someone's life or the history of some location. But here we are interested in the VOC rather than in Coen as a person, and for that matter in the VOC as an object changing stages through symbiosis rather than as an actor responsible for various events. Seen in this light, only three items on the list seem like good candidates to be termed symbioses. Two involve places, and are therefore reserved for the next section: the 1619 founding of Batavia as the VOC's regional capital, and the 1623 massacre in Ambon and resulting company dominance in the Spice Islands as a whole.

But for now we will focus on another possibly symbiotic moment: the 1614 submission of Coen's *Discourse on the State of India* to the so-called Heeren XVII, the corporate board of the VOC in Amsterdam. Moreover, only part of that treatise is of interest to us. Some of the *Discourse* addresses Dutch national security with respect to other European powers. Spain and Portugal are said to deserve no mercy, given their ongoing efforts to suppress Dutch political independence; thus Coen imagines a justified assault not only on the remaining Portuguese properties in the East Indies, but even on the Spanish in the

Philippines. England must also be forbidden to trade in the region so as to ensure the VOC's European monopoly on spices. None of this was entirely new. Verhoefen and his men were massacred in 1609 precisely because they wanted to enforce a monopoly on the spice trade in Banda. Even as far back as 1602, in the VOC's first year of existence, Captain Wolfert Harmenszoon had tried to enforce a contractual monopoly on the Spice Island of Neira that would have prevented the islanders from trading with their traditional Arab, Chinese, and Javanese partners, all of whom offered more useful goods in exchange than the Dutch (Brown 2009, 11–12). But Coen's treatise laid out a more systematic plan, as Brown notes:

> It was an absurdly ambitious vision, beguilingly wide in scope. [The VOC] bought into this intoxicating scheme, overlooking the unsavoury, though unspecified, violence needed to secure it. They now dreamed of dominating not only the Europe-Asia trade, but Asian inter-island shipping as well. (Brown 2009, 34)

Though Harmenszoon had brushed against a similar scheme, he had not made systematic claims on all local trade throughout the East Indies, and in practice the residents of Neira never took even his limited demands seriously. The symbiosis that transformed the VOC was its incorporation of Coen's treatise, which changed the company from an autonomous Dutch trade monopoly into a quasi-colonial extortion machine, its excesses rationalized by the existential peril otherwise faced by the young independent Netherlands.

Why do we date the first symbiosis from 1614 rather than 1621, when the document was first enacted in grisly fashion with massacre and enslavement in Banda? Because these atrocities merely announced the new VOC to the world through its effects, rather than constituting the new company. If the VOC had rejected Coen's document, he might still have carried out a revenge attack at Banda in the name of Verhoefen's ghost, but this would have been just a bloody and shameful one-off incident that might damage the VOC's reputation without expressing a new reality for it. Since an object must exist in order to act rather than act in order to exist, it follows that all objects have a greater or lesser period of *dormancy* prior to their first registering effects on the environment. An object or phase is born, and then there is a *lag* before it enters into relation with any outside object. A dormant object is one that is really present but without effect on other objects, or at least not yet.

In any case, rather than viewing the VOC as primarily an actor with effects, we have to see its actions as primarily an *aftershock* to its reality. The VOC is not what it does, but the widely discredited "what it is," not to be confused with the second duomining principle, "what it is made of." However momentous the actions of the newly Coenian VOC were to its neighbors, from the standpoint of the 1614 VOC these are merely incidents; in the terms of classical philosophy, they are *accidents*. To dismiss this dormant VOC as a worthless thing-in-itself, or as relevant only through the effects it eventually had, is to yield to a Whig history in which victory alone is what determines the reality of a thing: just as in the pre-1990s Hobbesian version of ANT. Any historical moment is populated not just with winners and losers, but also with still indeterminate pre-winners and pre-losers, and an ontology of the East Indies must consider these as well. Foremost among them at this stage was the EIC. Though actually founded two years earlier than the VOC, the EIC was a much weaker object at this point, due in part to the relative independence of each of its captains; Dale discovered as much when he failed to convince his nominal subordinates to pursue and destroy Coen's escaping fleet. There was also Portugal with its dwindling manpower and holdings, along with the nearly victorious Mataram Empire in Java, not to mention the lingering power of Aceh, Johore, Banten, China, and Japan. History has no choice but to recognize the greater success of some objects over others: of Romans over Etruscans, American Revolutionists over American Tories, and Atatürk's army of independence over the rejected Treaty of Sèvres. An immaterialist ontology departs from history in weighing an object's symbioses more heavily than the conflicts that weaken or destroy the enemy or the object itself.

One implication is that events are more dependent on objects than the reverse. Consider the Anglo-Dutch truce of 1619, which occurred against the background of the largely Catholic vs. Protestant Thirty Years' War (1618–48). By all expectations this truce should have counted as a decisive event, and even as the childhood death of Coen's maximalist VOC. Having been bewitched by Coen's dark treatise just five years earlier, the directors of the VOC were suddenly willing to hand over one-third of their spice trade to the already defeated English because of the political situation in Europe. Coen might easily have been cowed by this new situation, or simply decided that his own career was better served by obeying orders from Amsterdam. In that case the Coenian VOC would have died off, with a new non-Coenian VOC born through symbiosis with the truce, led either by a chastened Coen or a placid new Governor-General. Alternatively, it is possible that if Coen had died or resigned at this point, one of his deputies might have risen to the occasion like Augustus in the wake of his murdered uncle Julius, and taken as hard a line against the truce as did Coen himself. What actually happened is that Coen strangled the truce in its crib, craftily demanding military contributions from the English that he knew they were unable to provide. Once the population of Banda was ethnically cleansed, and especially once the English and others were massacred at Ambon, the truce-object was no longer viable, and the Coenian VOC was able to survive the death of one of its pivotal components: Coen himself.

Yet the creation of such *faits accomplis* must be assigned not to the birth of objects – since these must be born before they can win, lose, or do anything at all – but to the life-and-death struggle between already existing objects and stages: the Coenian VOC, the truce-VOC as envisaged in Amsterdam, the truce-EIC, and the independent Banda ruled by the numerous village chiefs or *orang kaya*. Since every object must try to establish "facts on the ground" in its early life-and-death struggles, it follows that most symbioses occur early in the life of an object, with a relatively enduring character established toward the end of that early period. Events cannot happen at just any moment, but are the aftershocks of the birth or new stage of an object.

Among other things, this explains why "great individuals" will usually be found clustered early in the history of their shared object, since opportunities for symbiosis arise most easily in the opening days of an object and its rivals. As already mentioned, important European philosophers almost always appear in bunches of three or four. Americans bemoan their mediocre politicians of today, who cannot compare with the dozen or so Founding Fathers who conducted

Revolution and ratified a Constitution between 1775 and 1787. The most illustrious political heroes of France grow in clumps during the Revolutionary and Napoleonic periods. German intellectual life is imprinted in perhaps permanent fashion by the *Sturm und Drang*, Romanticism, and Idealism of the 1700s–1800s, with Kant and Goethe the perhaps unrepeatable J. P. Coens of German intellectual history. Historians of science still gush over Ernest Rutherford's "heroic age of physics" (Rhodes 1986, 157) and its demigods such as Planck, Einstein, Bohr, Heisenberg, Schrödinger, and Rutherford himself, their achievements equaled by few if any scientists today. Such clusters of outstanding people are due not to the superior mental endowments and education of a given era, but to a briefly fermenting period of baby objects that need symbiosis with other objects to survive and flourish. The great object we now consider, if not great in the moral sense, was the Coenian VOC rather than Coen himself. Surely the VOC had other employees as cunning and ruthless as Coen at different points in its history. What such figures lacked was the right period of uncertain opportunity, and what the company would have lacked without Coen are his *Discourse* and his violent contempt for the 1619 Anglo-Dutch truce. We find no other person in VOC history who transformed the very reality of the company. If we seek "contingency" in history, this is not because any chance event might shift the course of history at any time, but only because of the sensitivity to different possible symbioses that prevails in an object's childhood.

9. Batavia, the Spice Islands, and Malacca

The spatial arena of the VOC was vast, with trade activities conducted not only in present-day Indonesia, but as far afield as Yemen and Iraq in the west and Japan, Taiwan, the Philippines, and Cambodia in the east. The VOC discovered Australia in 1606 and New Zealand in 1642, and would no doubt have traded extensively in those places if there were significant wealth to be gained. Obviously, not all points on the VOC map were of equal importance. Physical geography has always been even less democratic than the history of individuals; no egalitarian firebrand will insist that all *places* were created equal. The Ancient Egyptians seemed destined for greatness by the Nile, the British for sea power and liberalism by their status as a European island, and the French and Germans fated for land rather than sea prowess and for robust statism due to their placement in the midst of dangerous continental rivals. The geographical interpretation of history has long been pursued by political realists, and recently surged to public view once more with Jared Diamond's widely read *Guns, Germs, and Steel* (1999). However, all the examples just listed pertain to the *homeland* of any people, and thus to the geographical background of the *birth* of that people. By contrast, we are interested here in the symbioses of a company already anchored in Amsterdam before it came fully to grips with various key sites of the East.

The geography of the East Indies is fascinating and important, and deserving of a brief description here. Dominating the western approach to the region is the large island of Sumatra, shaped somewhat like the American state of Kentucky, but aligned from northwest to southeast. The northwestern tip of Sumatra was home to Aceh, an empire that long remained a thorn in the side of Europeans, while the island's western coast more generally was dotted with ports important for the pepper trade. Sumatra's proximity to two other pieces of land is what creates the two main choke-points in the region for any would-be imperial power. On its eastern side, Sumatra is close to the Malay Peninsula, occupied today by Thailand, Malaysia, and Singapore. The narrow body of water between the two is called the Strait of Malacca, named after the city whose strategic importance was clear to all powers in the region, and which was occupied for long periods by the Portuguese, Dutch, and English in succession. At the southeastern corner of Sumatra is the much shorter and narrower Sunda Strait, home to the deadly volcanic island of Krakatoa, and presenting another choke-point for commerce between Asia and Europe. Across the strait from Sumatra is the smaller Java, shaped roughly like Long Island and extending like that American isle along a straight west-east axis, trailed by a long archipelago with today's independent East Timor at its end. East of the Strait of Malacca is the island of Borneo, looking much like a bloated Cyprus and divided today like Cyprus between a north (Malaysia and tiny Brunei) and a south (Indonesia). East of Borneo is the Indonesian island Sulawesi (formerly Celebes), which looks uncannily like a humanoid snake or lizard. Heading eastward from Sulawesi one enters the Banda Sea, with its famous Spice Islands scattered between Sulawesi and New Guinea. In the Spice Islands we find such pivotal sites of the trade as Ambon in the south and the Moluccas in the north. Heading northward from the Spice Islands, one eventually reaches the Philippines, Taiwan, and Japan. Australia to the south played little role for the VOC except as a site of occasional exploration and shipwreck.

From all these historically fascinating sites, three in particular were of pivotal interest for the VOC. The first was the Spice Islands, then the only place in the world where nutmeg and mace (which come from the same fruit) could be found. These islands were also an excellent source of cloves, thus making these goods susceptible to monopoly trade at an outrageous markup. Even the less monopolizable cloves could be sold in Europe for as much as 25 times their purchase price (Burnet 2013, 109). This made these islands a perfect target for the monopoly that even the pre-Coenian VOC had in mind, and also marked them as the VOC's principal theater of cruelty. Other than the Spice Islands themselves, the most important places were the two aforementioned straits alongside Sumatra: the Strait of Malacca in the north and the Sunda Strait in the south. Since the Portuguese had been established in Malacca since 1511, the early Dutch presence was centered elsewhere: on the western end of Java near the Sunda Strait rather than in the north. Not until 1641 did the Dutch succeed in capturing Malacca as well, thereby linking the old Arab and Chinese trade routes into a single network (Parthesius 2010, 165).

Someone might also nominate Amsterdam, the home base of the company, as the fourth pivotal site of the VOC. But as already noted, though Amsterdam lies in the background of the VOC as a geographical mother ship, for this very reason it plays a role in the *birth* of the VOC but not in the later symbioses through which it transformed. The VOC's connection with Amsterdam is already too intimate for this city to enable the VOC to *change* once established. This idea has long been known to sociology as "the strength of weak ties" (Granovetter 1973). Close links such as those between family members, or the United States and Canada, provide a strong basis for financial, cultural, even emotional support, yet are so comfortable, close, and familiar as rarely to give rise to lucky breaks, promising risks, and major steps forward. Amsterdam must wish the VOC well, and can certainly provide advice and instruction, but the VOC's remote operations make it responsible for establishing its own constellation of new ties.

(a) Batavia

Of the three key places described above, the Dutch arrived first at the Sunda Strait, specifically at the long-established trade center of Banten on the northern coast of Java. This occurred before the VOC even existed, in the time of the so-called *Voor-Compagnieën*, or Pre-Companies. A Dutch expedition reached Banten in 1596 under the "arrogant and intemperate" Cornelis de Houtman, whose boorish demands got the Dutch off on the wrong foot in the East Indies, and who was unsurprisingly killed on his second journey to the region (Burnet 2013, 70). The Dutch found in Banten a thriving port dominated economically by Chinese, but filled also with Abyssinians, Arabs, Bengalis, Gujaratis, Spice Islanders, Turks, and others. They were also disturbed to find Portuguese in the city, though the Dutch would end Portugal's presence in Banten with a decisive early naval attack in 1601, the year before the VOC was founded.

In 1618, after the English gave refuge to some Portuguese escaped from Dutch custody, the Dutch and English skirmished in the streets of Banten. This convinced Coen that it was time to find a new capital for the VOC. After considering several options, he turned eastward to the young prince of Jayakarta, who wanted alliance with the Dutch to help end his subordinate status vis-à-vis Banten, and welcomed them to his city. This was viewed as a threat by both Banten and the English, who tried separately to put an end to the Dutch presence in Jayakarta. We saw earlier that these rivalries reached their climax in 1619 with Sir Thomas Dale's attack on the VOC and his ensuing failure to chase down and destroy Coen's fleet. We also saw that Coen returned to Jayakarta and treacherously defeated the very prince who had invited the VOC in the first place, renaming the city as a whole after its VOC fortress: "Batavia," the ancient Roman name for the Low Countries. After withstanding the aforementioned sieges by the Mataram Empire during Coen's second term, VOC Batavia was relatively secure. Only half a century later did the VOC see the wisdom and possibility of returning to conquer Banten itself. Following two years of warfare, that operation finally succeeded in 1684. As a result, "the English, French, and Danish [trading posts] in the city were closed" (Burnet 2013, 121), and once-important Banten was reduced to a protectorate, with Batavia the remaining seat of power in Java.

(b) The Spice Islands

The Dutch won the Spice Islands despite being relative latecomers. The Portuguese had been fascinated early by the legend of these islands, and after conquering Malacca in 1511, they sailed the next year for Ternate. Though they failed to arrive due to adverse winds, they were overjoyed to reach instead the Spice Island of Banda and its exotic nutmeg trees, and soon gained access to the entire region. After eventually building a fortress in Ternate and engaging in lucrative shipments to Lisbon for more than 50 years, the Portuguese found their monopoly eroded by smuggling and complex local politics. In 1570 this led them unwisely to murder the local Sultan Baabullah, whose son of the same name drove out the Portuguese five years later, becoming an anti-imperialist hero in the process. Even the English beat the Dutch to the area, when no less a figure than Sir Francis Drake arrived at Ternate in 1580. After crossing the Pacific with silver and gold pillaged from the Spanish Empire, he carried an already bulky cargo that prevented his loading spices as well. Nonetheless, Drake was greeted warmly by the younger Sultan Baabullah, who obtained his word of honor to return with an English fleet to drive the Portuguese from nearby Tidore. For various reasons, this did not occur anytime soon.

The Dutch did manage to visit the Spice Islands prior to the formation of the VOC, in 1598, under the commander Wybrand van Wawijk (Burnet 2013, 70–1). Reaching Ternate, they were greeted by the inquisitive Sultan Said, son and heir of the now deceased younger Baabullah. Impressed by the cannons of the VOC, Sultan Said invited them to join in attacking the Portuguese at Tidore, an offer van Wawijk was not then in a position to accept. But a heavier Dutch presence in the Spice Islands appeared in 1605, when the first full-blown VOC fleet arrived in the Spice Island of Ambon with orders to drive out the Portuguese for good. After a brief attack, the

Portuguese commander killed himself and his soldiers surrendered to the VOC, in an incident referred to by Burnet (2013, 98) as "the beginning of the decline of the Portuguese Estado da India."

Yet if the Dutch thought they had entered a military vacuum filled solely with Portuguese decline, they were wrong. The VOC's conquest of Ambon was witnessed by two English ships under Henry Middleton, who thereupon decided that rather than landing in Ambon itself, he would take one of his ships to Ternate for cloves while the other should sail to Banda in pursuit of nutmeg. Middleton happened to arrive in Ternate in storybook fashion: just in time to save the life of none other than Sultan Said, then in the midst of a losing naval battle with his rivals from Tidore. The grateful Said granted the British facilities on Ternate as well as clove-trading rights. He had not forgotten the pledge his father received years earlier from Sir Francis Drake to help Ternate attack the Portuguese at Tidore; thus the flames of alliance were rekindled. However, the Dutch quickly arrived with five ships of their own, which they also announced were there to meet Said's requests for assistance against the Portuguese. Said was now in a tricky diplomatic position, but found clever ways to play the Dutch, English, and Tidoreans off against each other while keeping his own hands clean. The upshot was that the VOC went on to attack the Portuguese fort in Tidore while the other parties remained on the sidelines. With the Dutch on the brink of defeat in the battle, they were saved by a gunpowder explosion (common in those years) that reduced the Portuguese fort to rubble. Having now conquered Ambon and Tidore, the VOC renovated and occupied an old Portuguese fort on Ternate in 1607. The company was now clearly the ascendant power in the Spice Islands. Yet there was still the unclear situation in Banda, as well as ongoing British rule over the rich Spice Islands of Ai and Run: the first English overseas possessions, with King James even styling himself "King of England, Scotland, Ireland, and Polo Run" (Burnet 2013, 104). But the Dutch soon applied themselves to completing the work of monopoly. In 1615 they attacked Ai, and were initially successful until their ranks were depleted by a surprise English counterattack, by night, from Run. In 1616 the Dutch returned in force, massacring the defenders of Ai and renaming the conquered English position with the bloodcurdling title "Fort Revenge." A small English force held out bravely in Run until their inevitable surrender in 1620. In the aftermath of their departure, a grim fate awaited the natives of Run: "the Dutch killed or enslaved every adult male, exiled the women and children, and then proceeded to chop down every nutmeg tree on the island, leaving behind a barren and uninhabited rock rising out of the Banda Sea" (Burnet 2013, 105). The dominance of the VOC in the Spice Islands was sealed by Coen's massacre of the Banda islanders in 1621 and van Speult's extermination of the English at Ambon in 1623.

There was another, long-lingering obstacle to a full VOC Spice Islands monopoly: the continued independence of the Sultanate of Macassar, located in the southwest of Sulawesi. Reputed in earlier years to be the homeland of pork-eaters and sodomites, Macassar by 1655 had become a reliable outpost of Islam under one Sultan Hasanuddin. Many of the Portuguese who fled the VOC conquest of Malacca in 1641 found protection in Macassar, which even welcomed the priests and the relics of Malacca Catholicism. More than this, Macassar was precisely the sort of free-trade port that the monopolist VOC had always tried to demolish: "Arab, Chinese, Portuguese, Spanish and English merchants frequented the port because the Sultan of Macassar allowed them to trade freely and outside Dutch control" (Burnet 2013, 130). The VOC blockaded Macassar in 1656, and again demanded monopoly in 1659, to which Sultan Hasanuddin replied firmly that God intended the earth for the enjoyment of all peoples, not just the Dutch. In response the VOC attacked the city in 1660, though conquest eluded them until 1669, "in what was described as some of the fiercest fighting ever experienced by the [VOC]" (Burnet 2013, 134). The resistant Sultan was exiled, and the VOC established total monopoly over the Spice Islands at last.

Given this ultimate state of monopoly, and the seven-decade economic boom for the VOC that followed, it is tempting to treat 1669 Macassar rather than 1623 Ambon as the moment of Spice Islands symbiosis. I am inclined to do the opposite for several reasons. The massacre of the English at Ambon marked the elimination of other European forces in the Spice Islands, aside from the various Portuguese exiles and assorted English and Spanish merchants living under Hasanuddin's protection. The fact that the Dutch made no effort to conquer Macassar until their 1656 blockade, more than 30 years after Ambon and 15 after the capture of Malacca, gives the VOC attack on Macassar the feel of a large and delayed mop-up operation rather than a pivotal transformation. Even the EIC seems to have written off the Spice Islands to VOC control as early as 1657. In that year, EIC Governor Sir William Cockayne actually proposed to sell off English properties throughout the region. His alarmingly pessimistic view of Dutch dominance in the East even startled Oliver Cromwell, who encouraged a redoubled focus on India and a commercial reorganization of the company (Burnet 2013, 140). Though both of these moves would prove decisive for England in the long run, at the time they seemed more like last-ditch salvage efforts. To summarize, the VOC's foes had more or less conceded the Spice Islands to Dutch control well before the 1669 conquest of Macassar. Thus we should read the capture of Macassar as an extrapolation of the 1623 Spice Islands VOC rather than a new turning-point, however vast the economic gains to which it led.

(c) Malacca

In 1557 the Portuguese received permission from the Chinese to settle in Macau, a place they would hold until distant 1999. Since the Portuguese also controlled strategic Malacca, they would naturally route their annual Macau trade through the Strait of Malacca en route to Goa and eventually Lisbon. This meant that the Dutch could have a destructive effect without even seizing Malacca outright: all they needed to do was harass or capture Portuguese ships on their approach to the Strait. In 1603 the VOC seized the Portuguese ship *Santa Catarina* near Johore: "The captured cargo was auctioned in Amsterdam for 3.5 million guilders, a profit which was said to have doubled the paid-up capital of [the] newly formed [VOC] in just one day" (Burnet 2013, 86). Much like the English after similar seizures of Portuguese vessels near the Azores and elsewhere, the Dutch were intoxicated by the size of these gains, and it was easy to assuage any feeling of shame over piracy by remembering that the Netherlands was still in a state of war with Portugal. In 1605 the Dutch made another lucrative capture of a Portuguese vessel, this time the *Santo António* near Thailand.

Under these circumstances the Portuguese in Malacca tried to make a deal with the Sultan of Johore, offering him military protection in exchange for the expulsion of VOC traders from his city. But it was too late for that: "The sultan replied that he would rather lose his entire kingdom than give in to such demands from the 'Enemies of Islam'" (Burnet 2013, 87–8). In effect, the Portuguese were paying a long-term price for Alfonso de Albuquerque's destruction of Islam in Malacca in 1511 and other provocative acts against the religion. Far from helping the Portuguese, the Sultan of Johore did the exact opposite, signing a treaty with the Dutch and agreeing to divide the spoils once Malacca was conquered. A first attempt in 1606 failed, with the VOC fleet somehow able to escape destruction by a Portuguese armada from Goa. A second attempt in 1608 under Pietrus Verhoefen also came to naught when the Dutch unluckily arrived during Ramadan: the Muslim army of Johore was unwilling to fight while fasting, and the luckless Verhoefen unknowingly sailed to his doom in Banda. Dutch harassment of Portuguese shipping continued for decades, with frequent blockades of Goa and Sri Lanka, not to mention the Strait of Malacca itself. In 1640 the Dutch assaulted Malacca for a third time, ordered there by VOC Governor-General Antonio van Diemen. Their fleet of 18 vessels exchanged cannon fire with the Portuguese fort, yielding no decisive result. But after a siege of five months led to obvious Portuguese attrition, the Dutch commander ordered a ground assault on the fort in 1641, and the Portuguese surrendered following brave resistance. The VOC now controlled both key straits in the region.

(d) General Reflections

The preceding pages have given a simplified version of the numerous conquests and trade missions that led to a sprawling VOC empire. Yet we are not concerned with all actions of the VOC-actor, but only with possible symbioses that changed its reality. To this end, the three places mentioned can be ranked as follows, in descending order of importance: Spice Islands, Sunda Strait, Strait of Malacca.

Dominance of the Spice Islands was essential for the wealthy but beleaguered Dutch, since lack of monopoly would have increased the local cost of spice while causing prices to plummet in

Europe through unwanted competition. Control of the islands also allowed the VOC to reach its Coenian goal of dominating intra-Asian trade. But what is the difference between Coen's maximalist 1614 VOC and the 1621–3 Spice Islands VOC? Since the situation in 1623 could be read as the natural outcome of Coen's 1614 treatise, perhaps the various Spice Islands victories could be dismissed as mere "incidents," the sorts of *actions* that immaterialist theory wants to de-emphasize by contrast with ANT and New Materialism. However, what makes 1623 different from many equally colorful dates is the difference between the aspiring and the actual conqueror. The maximalist VOC of 1623 differs from that of 1614 through its different internal constitution, shifting militarily from offensive to defensive procedures and mop-up operations, and in the midst of shifting commercially to an emphasis on Asia–Asia rather than Asia–Europe shipping routes. In this respect, 1623 is not merely the extrapolation of a plan from 1614, but a change in the company as a whole.

As for the two key straits in the region, they followed opposite trajectories in the life of the VOC. With Malacca initially in Portuguese hands, the VOC had little choice but to base its operations in Banten, then the main trade center in Java. They had no monopoly in Banten, of course, given the pluralist approach to trade prevailing in that port. The 50-mile move to Batavia gave the VOC breathing space for its operations, and the much later conquest of Banten by the VOC was more an anticlimactic expansion than a symbiosis changing the nature of the company. It was the opposite story with the Strait of Malacca, which the VOC initially used to damage the Portuguese rather than establish any foothold of its own. VOC dominance of the East Indies was attained even without possession of this key second strait. Yet the capture of Malacca in 1641 can still be considered symbiotic, through its importance in the tying together of the old Arab and Chinese trade routes. In short, the late conquest of Banten was a signal of its decline, while the late conquest of Malacca was a sign of its continued importance. Here there is also an interesting counterfactual question: what if the VOC had captured Malacca from the Portuguese in its attacks of 1606 or 1608 rather than failing to do so? Most likely, Batavia would never have been founded. The VOC could have based itself early in the Strait of Malacca, no doubt giving it a better chance of seizing Macau, forming symbiosis with Chinese trade, and increasing its chances of pre-empting the English in India as well. While this may have changed the character of the company in ways that never happened, such a company would still have been recognizably the VOC. Though we can only speculate about such non-occurrent events, the mere act of posing the counterfactual serves to remind us of a possible VOC-without-Batavia: along the lines of a Pasteur-without-hygienists (cf. Latour 1988), one who might have found some other way to implement his program. This cannot be accounted for by ANT, whose overemphasis on relations and effects would lead to an overidentification of the VOC with what *actually* happened to it.

10. The Intra-Asian VOC

We turn now to the third type of candidate noun for symbiosis: things. Perhaps the clearest such cases in history are found in the adoption of decisive new technologies: whether it be war chariots for the Indo-Europeans (Drews 1994), the telescope as employed by Galileo, Alan Turing's code-breaking machine, or the American atomic bomb. Yet symbiosis need not occur with technology, since it can occur just as easily with fish, disease, superstition, climate change, or most anything else. The first *things* that come to mind as pivotal for the VOC are the prized eastern spices that served as the blood of its operation. But here, as in the earlier case of Amsterdam, these spices belonged to the *birth* rather than the continued symbioses of the VOC, and thus belong to the "mother ship" category despite coming from distant lands. Spices gave birth to the VOC, but they no more transformed it than oil transforms Saudi Arabia today. Instead, these things are the subject of *strong* ties that, at most, can lead to the death of their possessors once they weaken or vanish: as when spices became less popular and less monopolizable in 1700s Europe, or at the still indefinite future date when Saudi oil is drained or unwanted.

One of the early problems faced by the VOC was that the people of the East Indies were generally not interested in the northern goods the Dutch had to offer: except precious metals, which the Dutch preferred not to send from Europe. Such standard Dutch merchandise as wool and lead was useless in the eyes of the Asians. This was another factor in the VOC aspiration to become more heavily involved in intra-Asian trade. Textiles from India were greatly valued by Spice Islanders and others, and thus the VOC established trade for these goods on the Coromandel Coast (on the eastern side of present-day India) as well as in Bengal, then under Mongol control. These textiles were often traded with Spice Islands natives for cloves. The VOC itself also frequently purchased Asian products for its own use: "Instead of wooden barrels, the VOC stored water and powder on the Spice Islands in *martabans* (*stoneware storage jars*) imported from ports in the Bay of Bengal" (Parthesius 2010, 53). The VOC conducted intra-Asian trade in rice, opium, horses, and silk, though it was slow to grasp the potential of an originally Ethiopian good we know today as coffee, quaintly described by the VOC's Pieter van den Broecke as "*Kahauwa*, a kind of black bean . . . of which [the Yemenis] make black water that they drink" (cited in Parthesius 2010, 46–7). Like its fellow stimulants chocolate and tobacco, coffee would later grow in importance, and the eventual EIC symbiosis with tea is one of the reasons it eclipsed the VOC in the 1700s when tea was on the rise and spice on the decline.

But while the types of goods needed to dominate intra-Asian trade changed the aims and geography of the VOC, an even greater change came through its symbiosis with a new type of fleet better adapted to the task of local dominance. Though the newborn VOC immediately abolished the practice of single-journey fleets disbanded upon return to the Netherlands, the early company continued to operate on the model of round-trip voyages between Europe and Asia. This required many large ships able to withstand the rigors of the journey, yet such massive vessels were not the best watercraft for entering shallow Asian ports and rivers. Given the dependence of return voyages on the regional pattern of monsoons, it would also be good to have a multi-tasking fleet that could change operations depending on circumstance. If this could happen, as it soon did, then the same vessel might be used one month for spur-of-the-moment trade opportunities, and the next as a gunboat for military operations: "For instance, the vessels from the [seasonal] Goa blockade could ship pepper from the Malabar Coast and cinnamon from Ceylon on their way

back to Batavia" (Parthesius 2010, 171). The
Dutch were legendary shipbuilders even before
the founding of the VOC, and they adapted to
the new situation with all the resourcefulness
one would expect. Furthermore, whenever possible the VOC attempted to build ships on-site
in Asia, and smaller ones at that, along with seizing suitable Portuguese or Chinese vessels for
their own use. All of this gave them a significant advantage over the other European powers:
"The developing complexity of the [VOC] trade
and shipping network between [various Asian]
regions illustrates the flexibility of the VOC in
utilizing the ships to the fullest extent and keeping them sailing, in contrast to the Portuguese
who often left ships idle in Macau, waiting for
a change of season" (Parthesius 2010, 57). The
reputation of the well-armed VOC fleet for
good security also made them the transporter of
choice for coinage circulating within Asia: "The
VOC was therefore effectively able to capitalize
on the exchange differences between gold and
silver values and between different kinds of coins,
by transporting large amounts of these curren-
cies" (Parthesius 2010, 57). Amusingly enough,
even corrupt English officials took to using the

VOC to transport their ill-gotten wealth back to Europe.

At first glance, it might seem difficult to link this shift to any specific year. But Parthesius does it with some precision, noting that even after the foundation of Batavia in 1619, "there was an interesting period of a few years during which the VOC hoped to concentrate on the transport of goods to Europe and leave most of [the] intra-Asian trade to the traditional and private European traders who would take the merchandise to Batavia" (Parthesius 2010, 31). This led to the closure of numerous facilities not directly linked to European trade, but the policy proved unsuccessful, so that "around 1625 the VOC had to return to their original set-up with a network of trading posts and strongholds to support strong intra-Asian trade" (Parthesius 2010, 32).

From all of this we see another way in which relational theories of objects often go wrong: they over-emphasize the links and alliances made by objects while neglecting to consider the ways that symbiosis *protects* an object from links, and thus further solidifies its autonomy. For example, Serial Endosymbiosis Theory surmises that a simple prokaryotic cell devoured a bacterium that survived by feasting on nutrients internal to that cell (Endosymbiosis 2008). When the cell later divided, the bacterium managed to divide as well, preserving its status as an element of all the heirs of the initial cell. Margulis predicted in the 1960s that evidence would be found that the DNA in the cell nucleus does not code for the various cell organelles, thereby proving their independent origin; in the 1980s, such evidence was indeed found. From this we learn both that eukaryotic cells were formed from multiple separate entities, and that the new and more complex cell became dependent on its organelles over time. But along with this obvious link, the new cell becomes *independent* of something else as well: the dangerous, newly oxygenated atmosphere. "The ingested bacteria ultimately performed oxidative metabolism necessary to the survival of the original host cell, which would otherwise have been poisoned by atmospheric oxygen" (Endosymbiosis 2008).

Thus it was for the VOC as well. The use of local Asian trade items and the construction of a fleet better suited for intra-Asian operations not only created stronger links between the VOC and alien Asian ports, but also further weakened its ties with Amsterdam. Note that this process not only served

Dutch commercial and military interests, but opened up new possibilities for Asian merchants themselves, such as abundant sales of pottery to the VOC and the hiring of its fleet for safe transport of precious metals. As long as the VOC traded goods primarily from home, as long as its business model was dominated by the round-trip voyages of large *retourschepen* ("return ships"), the intra-Asian reality of the VOC would be stifled. Yet this intra-Asian focus was not always healthy, as seen from the increasing involvement of VOC Governors-General in the wars among the Javanese following the conquest of Banten, a policy lamented by the Heeren XVII back home as unduly militaristic and wasteful (Burnet 2013, 137).

11. Touching Base Again with ANT

We have now reviewed just enough VOC history to venture some wider theoretical claims. Before moving in that direction, it will be helpful to explain once more what seems to be missing in the rival theory that is closest to the concerns of OOO. Although OOO is sometimes grouped with New Materialism, I have tried to show that OOO is a resolutely anti-materialist theory, whether we speak of traditional scientific materialism or of the more recent sorts of social constructionisms that call themselves materialist as well. Even more importantly, there is a tendency among the latter sort of materialism to deny the existence of individual objects in favor of a more primordial, vibrant continuum, described quite candidly by Jane Bennett as "the indeterminate momentum of the throbbing whole" (Bennett 2012, 226). The greatness of ANT, as I see it, consists largely in its return to individual entities as opposed to throbbing or static wholes, and in its willingness to allow all entities an equal claim to participating in its theory: human and non-human, natural and cultural, real and imaginary. This puts ANT in the ontologically democratic position once occupied by phenomenology, but without that school's excessive prioritizing of the observing human subject. Little wonder that such a powerful and flexible theory should have taken the social sciences by storm!

Yet despite being a great admirer of ANT, I believe that there are some problems with the theory, and the most significant of them may not be the ones conceded by Latour himself when he proclaims his "modes of existence" project as the solution to ANT's weaknesses (Latour 2013). One of the most over-cited lines of poetry among recent philosophers is surely Friedrich Hölderlin's "where the danger is, there too grows the saving power," now a tedious mantra among orthodox Heideggerians. Along with this phrase, we should also insist on the truth of its inversion: "where the saving power is, there too lies the danger." For ANT, as for so many theories, its moments of greatest insight are also its points of excess. I propose the following five ideas as belonging to ANT's greatest strengths and weaknesses simultaneously:

1. ANT *Pro*: "Everything is an actor."

The flat ontology of ANT allows it to avoid the modern dualist ontology in which all finite beings are implausibly divided between (a) people and (b) everything else. This is no small achievement in an era when many of the most popular thinkers are more enamored with the human subject than ever: Jacques Lacan, Alain Badiou, Slavoj Žižek, and Quentin Meillassoux come immediately to mind. ANT does better than these authors in its placing of all entities on an equal footing rather than assuming in advance that human beings are not just interesting, but are so utterly different in kind from everything else that they deserve an utterly different ontological category of their own. It is better to start by treating all things equally, so that any distinctions between them must be intellectually *earned* rather than smuggled in from the seventeenth century as purported self-evident truths. ANT does this even better than phenomenology did.

1. ANT *Contra*: "Why should *action* be the property that all entities have in common?"

We have already considered Aristotle's point that to say that someone is a house-builder only when they are currently building a house makes little sense. A person can build a house only because they are a house-builder, and not the reverse. More generally, a thing is capable of multiple actions and *for this very reason* need not perform any particular action, or any action at all. This is the classic OOO objection to relationist ontologies of every sort. In terms of practical method, the over-emphasis on the actions of an actor takes away our ability to ask counterfactual questions about it. If we measure authors, politicians, or wild animals by their degree of impact, then we erase missed opportunity, bad luck, and foolishness from our model of the world. Whether or not the practitioners of action-oriented social theories "know" that winners and losers do not always deserve their fates, any theory that overmines objects by paraphrasing them in terms of "what they do" has already conceded that history is a roster of winners, devoid of undeserved success and undeserved failure. If this were so, there would be no reason for Latour to rate Tarde above Durkheim, or for Whitehead to call John Locke the Plato of his era, views not universally shared. Although successful action is a good, rough symptom of the reality of an object, it is no more than rough and no more than a symptom. This is one reason to turn toward objects themselves rather than focusing even more on their actions and relations.

2. ANT *Pro*: "All relations are reciprocal."

Sir Isaac Newton's famous Third Law of Motion states that for every reaction there is an equal and opposite reaction. ANT incorporates a similar principle by considering minor entities as legitimate actors in their own right, rather than merely passive subalterns crushed by "powerful" entities. Left-wing critics of Latour, frustrated by his evident lack of interest in revolutionary politics, have not yet grasped the real basis of his indifference to revolution. It is not because Latour *respects* the existing power-relations in society, but rather because he *disrespects* them. For Latour, there is no power so great as to be immune from the fragility and reversibility that belong to every network. As he puts it in his brilliant appendix entitled *Irreductions*: "*We always misunderstand the strength of the strong.* Though people attribute it to the purity of an actant, it is invariably due to a tiered array of weaknesses" (Latour 1988, 201).

2. ANT *Contra*: "Many relations are not reciprocal at all."

Working in the spirit of Newton, action-based philosophies tend to see relations as occurring equally in both directions. This makes it difficult to understand those relations where dependence occurs primarily in one direction. The point is important, since a non-reciprocal concept of relation is needed not only to account for the Left's often justified complaints of exploitative relations (Bryant 2014, 197–211). It is needed as well to describe path-dependent relations in which "powerful" entities such as the VOC lose flexibility and mobility due to the strong ties that the archaeologist Ian Hodder has theorized under the term "entanglements" (Hodder 2012, 2014). To cite a simple example in the spirit of Hodder, Anthropocene civilization cannot easily rid itself of disposable plastic trinkets and their ultimate Pacific Ocean dumpyard, because too many jobs depend on such trinkets.

3. ANT *Pro*: "All relations are symmetrical."

Though this may sound the same as Point 2 above, it is really a subset of it, and one that could only be identified from an OOO standpoint. Let's assume that a given relation is reciprocal, meaning that both actors relate to each other. We will call this relation not just reciprocal, but also *symmetrical*, if both entities relate to each other in the same way: through an interaction of their respective qualities.

3. ANT *Contra*: "Not all relations are symmetrical."

OOO rejects the automatic symmetry of relations, because OOO is attentive to the split between objects and their qualities. Husserl's phenomenology made important use of this principle, by rejecting the old empiricist notion that an object is nothing more than a "bundle of qualities." Husserl reversed this philosophical cliché by insisting that we first experience an object, and continue to regard it as the same object even though its exact qualities continue changing from one moment to the next. A symmetrical relation is one where the qualities of one object interact with the qualities of another, while in asymmetrical relations it is an *object* that interacts with the qualities of another. A good example can be found in the difference between literal and metaphorical language. Consider the most famous recurring image of Homer: "wine-dark sea." Like all metaphors this one is not a strong tie, since there is nothing about the sea that immediately suggests wine, apart from their banal shared status as darkish liquids. If Homer had said "bluish-purple sea," or worse, "the sea which is a dark liquid just like wine," these might be accurate or strong literal descriptions, but by no means weak metaphorical ones. Yet calling the sea "wine-dark" not only ascribes wine's color and liquidity to the sea but also puts other, less

immediately relevant features of wine (intoxi-
cation, oblivion) into vague orbit around the
sea-object. The shared dark liquidity of the two
is merely a pretext for enabling the less plausible
wine-properties of the sea to go into effect. The
impossibility of "discursively" or "conceptually"
grasping this weak connection is precisely what
makes the metaphor powerful, in a way that the
more accurate "bluish-purple sea" is not. Proof
that the metaphor is non-reciprocal can be seen in
the fact that we are hearing "wine-dark sea" rather
than "sea-dark wine," which would be an entirely
different image. In this alternate case, *wine* would
be the object that vaguely acquires the properties
normally associated with the sea (navigability,
mystery, adventure, shipwreck, being filled with
monsters and sunken treasures). By contrast,
literal language *is* reciprocal: to make a non-
metaphorical comparison between two objects is
to detect similar properties shared by both. "A
crow is like a magpie" has informational but no
aesthetic value, since the comparison is too con-
vincing. "Amsterdam is like Venice" is a bit less
exact, though close enough that we still understand that literal information – most likely about
canals or maritime history – is being transmitted.

But to say "a hat is like a dolphin" is too long a throw for any metaphorical effect to take place. What is needed is the "sweet spot" where there is enough trivial resemblance between two things to put their less obvious resonance into play.

4. ANT *Pro*: "All relations are equally important."

One of the great theoretical advantages of ANT is its ability to treat all actions as equally actions. Napoleon crowning himself Emperor in 1800 is an action, but so is the trivial dripping of candle wax onto a paper plate in some wretched attic apartment. The same equivalence holds both for Napoleon crowning himself and Napoleon coughing once or twice on an insignificant day. This equivalence performs just the sort of initial flattening that any philosophy needs in order to dispel traditional presuppositions.

4. ANT *Contra*: "All relations are not equally important."

In our discussion of symbiosis, the case was already made that not all actions are equal. There are trivial moments in the life of an object, and then there are moments of symbiosis that transform the very reality of that object. ANT's insensitivity to this point leaves it with no way to distinguish important and unimportant moments other than by granting special importance to noisy external impacts on the environment. But with symbiosis, we are speaking of a moment that is important primarily to an object, not to its environment. More generally, ANT's relative inability to distinguish between important and unimportant events leaves it unable to shed any light on the life-cycle of an object. In a sense the point is moot anyway, since by overidentifying an actor with its sum total of relations in any instant, ANT does not really allow for the existence of "the same" object over time. In the strict sense, Latourian actors (like their forerunner, Whitehead's "actual entities") last only for an instant, and are replaced in the following instant by a similar but not identical actor.

5. ANT *Pro*: "We cannot distinguish between different types of entities."

Latour does relapse somewhat into a modern human/nonhuman duality in his "modes" project, where the modes are classified according to their respective relations to "quasi-objects" and "quasi-subjects" (Latour 2013). Nevertheless, the flat ontology found in *Irreductions* (Latour 1988) requires that we treat all things as actors, without drawing rigid taxonomical distinctions between them.

5. ANT *Contra*: "We must distinguish between different types of entities."
Ultimately, any theory worth its salt needs to shed light on the difference between humans, nonhumans, natural entities, cultural entities, technologies, flowers, mammals, and so forth. Latour's recent attempts to draw such distinctions between different modes of existence are yielding interesting results, but do not even attempt to draw distinctions between types of actors. This remains an item of unfinished business for ANT.

To summarize, OOO holds that: (1) entities are partially withdrawn objects rather than merely public actors, (2) relations between objects may be non-reciprocal, (3) relations between objects may be asymmetrical, (4) there is a difference between the important and unimportant relations of an object, and (5) one of the tasks of philosophy is to find a new way to classify different types or families of objects. Before trying to derive some related principles from these five points, there is more to be said about the company that ruled the East Indies from Amsterdam.

12. Birth, Ripeness, Decadence, and Death

The conclusion above was that, amidst the countless dramatic incidents in its history, the VOC underwent just five symbioses that transformed the reality of the company. These were as follows:

- 1614: Coen's *Discourse on the State of India*
- 1619: The founding of Batavia as the VOC capital
- 1623: Massacre in Ambon and resultant dominance of the Spice Islands
- 1625: The VOC is reoriented toward intra-Asian trade
- 1641: The conquest of Malacca from the Portuguese ties together the old Arab and Chinese trade routes

Having tried to identify these moments of symbiosis in the life of the VOC, we should try to pinpoint the moments of its birth, its rise and fall, and finally its death, in order to consider what makes each of these moments so different in structure.

The birth of the VOC is intriguing in its own right. In 1580, King Philip of Spain laid claim to the vacant throne of Portugal. The two countries were thereupon united and would remain so until 1668, though their overseas possessions remained separate. In 1581, the Dutch rebelled against Spanish Hapsburg rule and formed the independent United Provinces of the Netherlands under the leadership of the House of Orange. Since a state of war now existed between the Netherlands and the combined Iberian power, Dutch ships were banned from Lisbon. This severely depleted the spice trade in Amsterdam and Antwerp, which had flourished due to Dutch maritime prowess and extensive commercial networks in northern Europe along with easy access to Portugal. If the Dutch wanted to continue their lucrative spice trade, they now had no choice but to do it all themselves, under newly dangerous conditions. Encouragement came from the publication of Jan Huygen van Linschoten's *Itinerario* in 1592. Previously employed for 11 years by the Portuguese in Goa, van Linschoten never ventured further than that city, but diligently collected information about all points further east. Along with his detailed descriptions of the flora and geography of the East Indies, he shared navigational and commercial secrets furtively copied from Portuguese records in Goa, and gave "a frank account of the Portuguese, their greed, divisiveness and lack of organization," and thereby "undermined the myth of Portuguese invincibility in the region" (Burnet 2013, 69). Just one year later, a group of Dutch merchants commissioned a map of the East Indies, and the ill-fated Cornelis de Houtman was somehow able to make a fact-finding journey to Lisbon. He was appointed commander of the first Dutch voyage to Banten in 1595, arriving as we have seen the next year. There followed a number of separate Dutch voyages to the region, until it became obvious that the various expeditions were undercutting each other by driving down market prices. The chosen solution was to force all Dutch East India traders to operate in a unified company, though the plan met initial resistance from the various Dutch regions or "Chambers," each jealous of its independence. Their reluctance was addressed in 1602 by the establishment of the VOC with a governing body known as the Heeren XVII: eight merchants representing Amsterdam, four from Middelburg, and one apiece from Delft, Enkhuizen, Hoorn, and Rotterdam. A tie-breaking seventeenth member rotated between cities other than Amsterdam, in order to prevent that powerful metropole from ever holding an automatic majority. The first unified VOC fleet was sent in December 1603, and we have seen that in 1605 it captured the Portuguese fort at Ambon.

We now consider the ripening of the VOC. Earlier, I argued that the VOC reached its mature form as an object with the 1641 capture of Malacca. There were further steps forward in both the financial and the military sense, but we can view these as part of the expansion of the VOC rather than a further set of symbioses. The first was the 1669 conquest of Macassar, which gave the VOC a more complete monopoly over the Spice Islands than obtained in 1623 at Ambon: "For the next 70 years [after Macassar was conquered] the [VOC] delivered continuous profits to its shareholders and it became the most powerful trading company the world had ever seen" (Burnet 2013, 136). But between 1670 and 1700, Burnet reports, the total market share in Amsterdam of cloves and fine spices among all imported products had dropped from 59 percent to 35 percent, an alarming sign given that spices were the VOC's monopolist specialty. Meanwhile, the share of Indian textiles rose during the same period from 29 percent to 44 percent, and Indian products were England's strong suit rather than the VOC's. Meanwhile, "tea and coffee [increased] from almost nothing to 25[%]" (Burnet 2013, 136), another good sign for England: especially as concerns tea, given their greater access to China. Other commercial threats emanated from the Western Hemisphere: "Vegetables from the New World such as corn, potatoes, tomatoes and chili peppers were adding variety to people's diets. The competition from new sources of cloves and nutmeg, smuggled out of the East Indies by Pierre Poivre and entering the market from the French colonies, was another difficulty" (Burnet 2013, 136).

The decline of the VOC was not far off. Things gradually became worse following the turn of the century: "the Dutch wars with France had increased the national debt and the [Dutch]

Republic allowed its fleets to deteriorate until by 1720 Britain replaced Holland as the dominant maritime power of the world" (Burnet 2013, 137). There was no immediate VOC collapse, though one gets the sense in this period of a company that is no longer hungry but merely trying to hold on to what it already has. The VOC's 1759 attack on the English in Calcutta was ineptly planned and executed, and so thoroughly crushed by Colonel Francis Forde's army, that "only sixteen Europeans [out of 700] were able to escape the battle alive and reach the Dutch [trading post] at Chinsurah" (Burnet 2013, 145). Even so, the VOC managed some gains during this period, as objects often do even in their decline. There was a 1722 monopoly deal on tin with the Buginese who now controlled Johore, with Tanjung Pinang near modern Singapore becoming the chief harbor in the area. The VOC even had a good year as late as 1784. After cheating Raja Haji of the Riau Islands of his rightful share of some opium looted jointly from the English, the VOC engaged in further deceit and attempted a pre-emptive strike against him. This ended disastrously, with the VOC flagship destroyed in yet another powder explosion. Raja Haji thereupon attacked and surrounded Malacca, and victory for the Buginese seemed near. Yet just then, a small but powerful fleet appeared at Malacca, one belonging to the actual Dutch Navy (!) rather than the VOC. This naval force landed soldiers near the invaders, captured their fortress, and killed Raja Haji. From there they turned to Tanjung Pinang, where they slaughtered an outnumbered force of Buginese. As a result, the Dutch were conceded a fortress in Riau. Nonetheless, the VOC's military dependence on the Dutch Navy in surviving a key Asian battle was an ominous sign of decay in the company itself.

The end came quickly for the VOC, like a hard rain. The Dutch had become too involved with the American Revolution, preceded only by France in recognizing the independence of the Thirteen Colonies. As a result, England blockaded the ports of the Netherlands from 1780 through 1784, leading to grievous economic harm. Early in this period, "the VOC called an 'extraordinary' meeting [in 1781] . . . The Compagnie credibility was at risk because the Hoorn Chamber could not meet a repayment demand" (Burnet 2013, 138). The Dutch government refused to bail out the VOC, and the Hoorn Chamber defaulted, damaging the

VOC's credibility. The rise of France intervened in the life of the VOC as well, when Napoleon invaded the Netherlands in 1794 and sacked the government the next year, with the French flag raised over Batavia a dozen years later. A surging England began to chip away at the VOC's holdings, capturing Malacca in 1795 and Ambon in 1796. In the meantime, the VOC found itself bankrupt and nationalized, converted into an organelle of the Dutch colonial authority. Though Batavia, Malacca, and Ambon would change their European claimants several times in the coming decades through treaty and combat, the VOC no longer existed to regain its former possessions.

13. Fifteen Provisional Rules of OOO Method

Though a longer book would be needed to apply the OOO method in full, we know enough by now to conclude with a series of 15 provisional rules, derived in large part from our discussion of the VOC.

Rule 1: *Objects, not actors*
Things pre-exist their activity rather than being created by it. The VOC is not the VOC because

it conquers the Spice Islands, but conquers the Spice Islands because it is the VOC. The military operations in Ambon, Ternate, Tidore, Ai, and Run are not random isolated events gathered together by a nicknamed pseudo-substance, but make sense only for a pre-existent entity conceptualized as a monopoly within the Netherlands, then at the expense of other European powers, and finally extended to trade within Asia itself.

Rule 2: *Immaterialism, not materialism*

In both its classic and present-day forms, materialism is a program for "cutting to the chase" and replacing objects by their composition or their outward effects. Yet we have seen that objects often gain the upper hand over their own constituent pieces, and can even abstain from any action at all, whether willingly or not. If Coen had been slain by Dale's fleet at Jayakarta in 1619, the Coenian VOC would probably have died young as well. Though now a paper project rather than one with external historical impact, it does not fall into the cracks of non-being. Though history is unkind to failed objects, ontology must affirm their reality.

Rule 3: *An object is better known by its non-relations than its relations*

Whereas ANT tends to view non-relational objects as isolated failures, immaterialism sees the stages of an object as being primarily steps toward autonomy rather than interconnectivity. The VOC is an especially good example of this, since its history does not show increasing attempts from Amsterdam to rein it in, as might have happened if electronic communication were somehow invented in the seventeenth or eighteenth century. Instead, we see a movement of the VOC toward ever-greater autonomy, at least until the Dutch Navy has to save it from the Buginese invasion of Malacca.

Rule 4: *An object is better known by its proximate failures than by its successes*

Whereas ANT asks us to look for alliances that make an actor stronger, immaterialism holds that the weaknesses of an object are often more important. I say "proximate" failures because it would be absurd, for instance, to ridicule the VOC for not making the first landing on the moon. Too many intermediate objects lie between the death of the VOC in 1795 and the successful Apollo mission in 1969. We should look instead for the neighboring failures that were not a foregone conclusion. It is conceivable that the VOC might one day have gained the upper hand in Japan or China – though these adversaries turned out to be much too strong – and conceivable as well that it might have emerged victorious in Calcutta and Macau, both places where it failed badly in military terms. These failures shed light on the permanent gap between the principle of unlimited VOC expansionism and the factors constraining its infinite continuation. They also give rise to "ghost" objects that offer fuel for endless counterfactual speculation, not all of it worthless.

Rule 5: *The key to understanding social objects is to hunt for their symbioses*

The first VOC symbiosis is one we have not yet discussed. Early in the company's history, as costs and troubles increased in the East Indies, the Heeren XVII took the important step of establishing a Council of the Indies in Banten, led by a new officer to be called the Governor-General. The first, Pieter Both, took up work in 1610; the infamous Coen would serve as the fourth and sixth. This creation of the Governor-General's position deserves to be regarded as a further symbiosis, since it increased the VOC's autonomy from the Dutch homeland, setting the table for Coen's full-fledged rebellion against the truce with the EIC. Thus we should add 1610 to our previous list: 1614 (Coen's treatise), 1619 (Batavia), 1623 (Ambon), 1625 (intra-Asian fleet), and 1641 (Malacca), giving us exactly a half-dozen, though this number may vary somewhat in other cases.

Rule 6: *Symbioses will occur relatively early in the life of an object*
Many social objects meet with a quick death, as nearly happened to the Coenian VOC in 1619. For those that survive, the window of growth will be relatively short even if the object's survival is long. From the list above, we have six symbioses occurring in the first four decades of the VOC's existence. These will tend to make an object sufficiently path-dependent that the space of options decreases. After 1641, the VOC is so strongly linked with commerce requiring a monopoly on certain spices, so beholden to shareholders expecting continued dividends, and

so surrounded by enemies and rivals, that a radical change in the VOC's business model would no longer be possible. Thus the mortality of the VOC comes into view, even as its profits and victories increase for decades to come.

Rule 7: *Symbiosis is not infinitely flexible once an object's character is established*

Every social object has a point of no return beyond which its possible courses of action narrow drastically in scope. I am inclined to view 1623 as the VOC's point of no return. The company's maximalist program can no longer be retracted after the massacre of the English at Ambon; it is now committed to aggressive monopoly against Europeans and Asians alike.

Rule 8: *Symbioses are weak ties that mature into strong ones*

The first strong ties of an object are those that exist from the moment of its birth. This is why Amsterdam, certain exotic spices, and general Dutch maritime skill are part of the initial "mother ship" of the VOC rather than factors in its further development, while the initially weak ties with Batavia, Indian textiles, and an intra-Asian fleet plan enable symbioses. The laws of efficiency require that we form ever closer links with our various organelles. What begins as an experimental and adventurous symbiosis ends up as a hyper-dependent bond that puts the very life of an object at risk. The VOC's strong tie with the Spice Islands becomes a path-dependent burden that undercuts the VOC once spices lose popularity or spread to the French Caribbean colonies.

Rule 9: *Symbioses are non-reciprocal*
Our paradigm case of reciprocal interaction came from Newton and his law stating that "every action has an equal and opposite reaction." Symbiosis is not like this. One object can form ties with another without the latter forming any tie with the first at all. Consider the astronomer's link with the Andromeda Galaxy, which at millions of light years from Earth cannot have any current relation with *homo sapiens*. In other cases, such as the VOC's relationship with Bandanese culture, the latter does not undergo symbiosis but rather outright destruction at the hands of the stronger object. While two objects may symbiose with each other simultaneously, such as the

VOC with Coen and Coen with the VOC, these are still different symbioses. "Wine-dark sea" is not "sea-dark wine," not even if Homer had used them both in the same stanza.

Rule 10: *Symbioses are asymmetrical*
Symmetrical relations are those in which objects are brought together by shared features or interests. Consider, for example, the formation of the G7 in 1976 by a number of wealthy and powerful democracies: Great Britain, France, West Germany, Italy, Japan, the United States, and Canada. There is obviously a strong link between these countries, just as there is between the 28 countries of today's European Union. It is often complained that such entities are futile as sources of change, but that is precisely the point: the ties are deliberately strong, meant to generate stability rather than motion. I would say the same of the 193 members of today's United Nations. While it might be thought that these vastly different countries do not have enough in common to make for a useful body, the truth is that their ties are *too* strong, in accordance with the lowest common denominator of sovereignty. The United Nations is a stabilizing organization by design.

A more asymmetrical relation can be found in the G7's expansion in 1998 to include Russia, whose relative weakness at the time allowed its rather different features and national interests to enter the group with relatively little worry. But growing oil wealth and the harder policy of Vladimir Putin helped bring Russia's differences to the fore in Georgia and then Ukraine: making for an asymmetry that the non-symbiotic G7 was never meant to incorporate, with Russia's membership suspended accordingly.

Rule 11: *Objects as events are echoes of objects as objects*

Some years ago, I happened to see a television documentary about the personal computer revolution wrought by Apple and Microsoft. One interviewee in the film made a seemingly innocent remark about American popular culture: "You have to remember that the 1960s really happened in the 1970s." The point of the remark seemed to be that an object somehow exists "even more" in the stage following its initial heyday. The marijuana smoking, free love, and internal violence of the dramatic American 1960s were in some ways even better exemplified by the

campy and tasteless 1970s. So too, the maximalist VOC already exists in Coen's treatise of 1614,
though it seems to exist "even more" nearly a
decade later, when the Spice Islands are violently
gathered under its yoke. As we might say: "You
have to remember that Coen's 1614 treatise really
happened in 1623."

Rule 12: *The birth of an object is both reciprocal
and symmetrical*

In Rule 10 we saw that a literal group based on
common interests, like the G7, is not itself an
adventurous symbiosis but a stabilizing mecha-
nism. On this basis we can see that the birth of
the VOC was not a symbiosis between the different chambers, but an enforced literal compromise
based on the common interests of Amsterdam,
Delft, Enkhuizen, Hoorn, Middelburg, and
Rotterdam. All were Dutch-speaking maritime
cities with a vested interest in high prices for their
goods. All were linked by the same laws, even if
the greater power of Amsterdam and Middelburg
led to their receiving more representatives in the
Heeren XVII. The birth of an object means less
autonomy in exchange for greater efficiency, while
symbiosis means more autonomy in exchange for

greater risk and possibly even greater reward. The birth of a social object is governed by the spirit of advantage rather than the spirit of adventure, while with symbiosis the reverse holds true.

Rule 13: *The death of an object arises from the excessive strength of its ties*

The VOC did not expire due to the weakness of its links with Malacca, Ambon, Batavia, nutmeg, or mace, but because of the excessive strength of those ties. Strong ties mean dependence, and that means devastation when one of these ties is suddenly weakened: as with the falling profit of spice in the 1700s, or the growing vulnerability of Malacca to attack and consequent reliance on the Dutch Navy for security.

Rule 14: *The ripening of an object comes from the expansion of its symbioses*

In its eastern region, the symbioses of the VOC were complete in 1623 with the seizure of Ambon. Its conquest of holdout Macassar in 1669 was an expansion of the symbiosis of 1623 rather than a new symbiosis, given that general VOC ownership of the Spice Islands was largely uncontested after 1623. Once an object's symbioses are complete, generally within a few decades after its birth, it can expand, decline, or die, but not enter a new stage.

Rule 15: *The decadence of an object comes from the literalization of its symbioses*

In the arts or philosophy we speak of decadence when the vague guiding innovations of a success-ful movement are reduced to formulae that any hack can utilize. Consider the representational "academic art" that reigned in Paris while Picasso and Matisse were still obscure young laughing stocks. Consider, too, the hack late Abstract Expressionist painting of early 1960s New York, or the hack Cubism within reach of any Sunday painter today. We might also recall the later years of German Idealism, phenomenology, decon-struction, or any philosophical movement that has already crested. Authors try to "sound" like Husserl, Derrida, or Deleuze, repeating their verbal and conceptual mannerisms though no longer in contact with the genuine dangers faced by these thinkers. This is the sound of decadence. Here we see why constant innovation is needed: not as an empty play of fashion that drowns out the mastery of perennial truth (as conservatives have it), and not as the endless production of new commodities whose blood can be sucked by vampiric capitalism (as the Left has it), but because any object eventually turns into a caricature of itself: an easily mastered literal content that can easily be mimicked.

Let this serve as a compact list of the first principles of object-oriented social theory, which I have also called "immaterialism" because of the hopelessly duomining character of every form of materialism.

References

Aristotle (1999) *Metaphysics*, trans. J. Sachs. Santa Fe,
  NM: Green Lion Press.

Badiou, Alain (2006) *Being and Event*, trans.
  O. Feltham. London: Continuum.

Barad, Karen (2007) *Meeting the Universe Halfway:
  Quantum Physics and the Entanglement of Matter
  and Meaning*. Durham, NC: Duke University
  Press.

Bennett, Jane (2012) "Systems and Things: A Response
  to Graham Harman and Timothy Morton," *New
  Literary History* 43(2), 225–33.

Brooks, Cleanth (1947) *The Well Wrought Urn: Studies
  in the Structure of Poetry*. Orlando, FL: Harcourt,
  Brace & Co.

Brown, Stephen R. (2009) *Merchant Kings: When*

Companies Ruled the World: 1600–1900. New York: Thomas Dunne Books.

Bryant, Levi R. (2011) "The Ontic Principle," in Levi R. Bryant, Nick Srnicek, & Graham Harman (eds), *The Speculative Turn: Continental Materialism and Realism*. Melbourne: re.press, pp. 261–78.

Bryant, Levi R. (2014) *Onto-Cartography: An Ontology of Machines and Media*. Edinburgh: Edinburgh University Press.

Burnet, Ian (2013) *East Indies: The 200 Year Struggle between the Portuguese Crown, the Dutch East India Company and the English East India Company for Supremacy in the Eastern Seas*. Kenthurst, Australia: Rosenberg Publishing.

Clulow, Adam (2014) *The Company and the Shogun: The Dutch Encounter with Tokugawa Japan*. New York: Columbia University Press.

Coole, Diana & Samantha Frost (eds) (2010) *New Materialism: Ontology, Agency, and Politics*. Durham, NC: Duke University Press.

DeLanda, Manuel (2006) *A New Philosophy of Society*. London: Continuum.

Deleuze, Gilles & Claire Parnet (2002) *Dialogues II*, trans. B. Habberjam, E. R. Albert, & H. Tomlinson. New York: Columbia University Press.

Diamond, Jared (1999) *Guns, Germs, and Steel: The Fates of Human Societies*. New York: Norton.

Drews, Robert (1994) *The Coming of the Greeks: Indo-European Conquests in the Aegean and the Near East*. Princeton, NJ: Princeton University Press.

Eldredge, Niles & Stephen Jay Gould (1972) "Punctuated Equilibria: An Alternative to Phyletic Gradualism," in Thomas J. M. Scopf (ed.), *Models in Paleobiology*. New York: Doubleday, pp. 82–115.

Endosymbiosis (2008) "Endosymbiosis: Serial Endosymbiosis Theory (SET)," blog post. Available at: http://endosymbionts.blogspot.com. tr/2006/12/serial-endosymbiosis-theory-set.html

Granovetter, Mark S. (1973) "The Strength of Weak Ties," *American Journal of Sociology* 87(6), 1360–80.

Harman, Graham (2009) *Prince of Networks: Bruno Latour and Metaphysics*. Melbourne: re.press.

Harman, Graham (2010a) *Towards Speculative Realism: Essays and Lectures*. Winchester, UK: Zero Books.

Harman, Graham (2010b) "Time, Space, Essence, and Eidos: A New Theory of Causation," *Cosmos and History* 6(1), 1–17.

Harman, Graham (2011) *The Quadruple Object*. Winchester, UK: Zero Books.

Harman, Graham (2012a) "On the Supposed Societies of Chemicals, Atoms, and Stars in Gabriel Tarde," in Godofredo Pereira (ed.), *Savage Objects*. Lisbon: INCM, pp. 33–43.

Harman, Graham (2012b) *The Third Table/Der dritte Tisch*, Documenta (13) Notebooks series, ed. K. Sauerländer, German version trans. B. Hess. Ostfildern, Germany: Hatje Cantz Verlag.

Harman, Graham (2013) "Undermining, Overmining, and Duomining: A Critique," in J. Sutela (ed.), *ADD Metaphysics*. Aalto, Finland: Aalto University Design Research Laboratory, pp. 40–51.

Harman, Graham (2014a) *Bruno Latour: Reassembling the Political*. London: Pluto Press.

Harman, Graham (2014b) "Conclusions: Assemblage Theory and its Future," in Michele Acuto and Simon Curtis (eds), *Reassembling International Theory: Assemblage Thinking and International Relations*. London: Palgrave Macmillan, pp. 118–31.

Harvey, Penny, Eleanor Conlin Casella, Gillian Evans, Hannah Knox, Christine McLean, Elizabeth B. Silva, Nicholas Thoburn, & Kath Woodward (eds) (2013) *Objects and Materials: A Routledge Companion*. London: Routledge.

Hodder, Ian (2012) *Entangled: An Archaeology of the*

Relationship Between Humans and Things. Oxford: Wiley.

Hodder, Ian (2014) "The Entanglements of Humans and Things: A Long-Term View," *New Literary History* 45, 19–36.

Johnston, Adrian (2013) "Points of Forced Freedom: Eleven (More) Theses on Materialism," *Speculations* IV, 91–8.

Kant, Immanuel (2003) *Critique of Pure Reason*, trans. N. K. Smith. New York: Palgrave Macmillan.

Knorr Cetina, Karin (1997) "Sociality with Objects: Social Relations in Postsocial Knowledge Societies," *Theory, Culture & Society* 14(4), 1–30.

Latour, Bruno (1988) *The Pasteurization of France*, trans. A. Sheridan and J. Law. Cambridge, MA: Harvard University Press.

Latour, Bruno (1993) *We Have Never Been Modern*, trans. C. Porter. Cambridge, MA: Harvard University Press.

Latour, Bruno (1996) "On Interobjectivity," trans. G. Bowker, *Mind, Culture, and Activity: An International Journal* 3(4), 228–45.

Latour, Bruno (1999a) "On Recalling ANT," in John Law & John Hassard (eds), *Actor Network Theory and After*. London: Wiley-Blackwell.

Latour, Bruno (1999b) *Pandora's Hope: Essays in the*

Reality of Science Studies. Cambridge, MA: Harvard University Press.

Latour, Bruno (2007) "Can We Get Our Materialism Back, Please?," *Isis* 98, 138–42.

Latour, Bruno (2013) *An Inquiry into Modes of Existence: An Anthropology of the Moderns*, trans. C. Porter. Cambridge, MA: Harvard University Press.

Latour, Bruno & Steve Woolgar (1986) *Laboratory Life: The Construction of Scientific Facts*. Princeton, NJ: Princeton University Press.

Law, John (2004) *After Method: Mess in Social Science Research*. New York: Routledge.

Leibniz, G. W. (1989) "Monadology," in *Philosophical Essays*, trans. R. Ariew and D. Garber. Indianapolis, IN: Hackett.

Margulis, Lynn (1999) *Symbiotic Planet: A New Look at Evolution*. New York: Basic Books.

Marres, Noortje (2005) "No Issue, No Public: Democratic Deficits After the Displacement of Politics," PhD dissertation, University of Amsterdam, The Netherlands. Available at: http://dare.uva.nl/record/165542

Meillassoux, Quentin (2008) *After Finitude: Essay on the Necessity of Contingency*, trans. R. Brassier. London: Continuum.

Meillassoux, Quentin (2012) "Iteration, Reiteration, Repetition: A Speculative Analysis of the Meaningless Sign" (a.k.a. "The Berlin Lecture"), trans. R. Mackay, unpublished manuscript. Available at: https://cdn.shopify.com/s/files/1/0069/6232/files/Meillassoux_Workshop_Berlin.pdf

Mol, Annemarie (2002) *The Body Multiple: Ontology in Medical Practice*. Durham, NC: Duke University Press.

Mol, Annemarie & John Law (1994) "Networks and Fluids: Anaemia and Social Topology," *Social Studies of Science* 24(4), 641–71.

Parthesius, Robert (2010) *Dutch Ships in Tropical Waters: The Development of the Dutch East India Company (VOC) Shipping Network in Asia: 1595–1660*. Amsterdam: Amsterdam University Press.

Pseudo-Dionysius (1987) *Pseudo-Dionysius: The Complete Works*, ed. by Colm Lubheid. Mahwah, NJ: Paulist Press.

Rhodes, Richard (1986) *The Making of the Atomic Bomb*. New York: Simon and Schuster.

Sagan, Lynn (1967) "On the Origin of Mitosing Cells," *Journal of Theoretical Biology* 14(3), 225–74.

Stengers, Isabelle (2010) *Cosmopolitics I*, trans. R. Bononno. Minneapolis, MN: University of Minnesota Press.

Tarde, Gabriel (2012) *Monadology and Sociology*, trans. T. Lorenc. Melbourne: re.press.

Willis, John E. Jr. (2005) *Pepper, Guns, and Parleys: The Dutch East India Company and China: 1662–1681*. Los Angeles, CA: Figueroa Press.

Zubíri, Xavier (1980) *On Essence*, trans. A. R. Caponigri. Washington, DC: Catholic University of America Press.